BY ERIC RIPERT

SEAFOOD SIMPLE

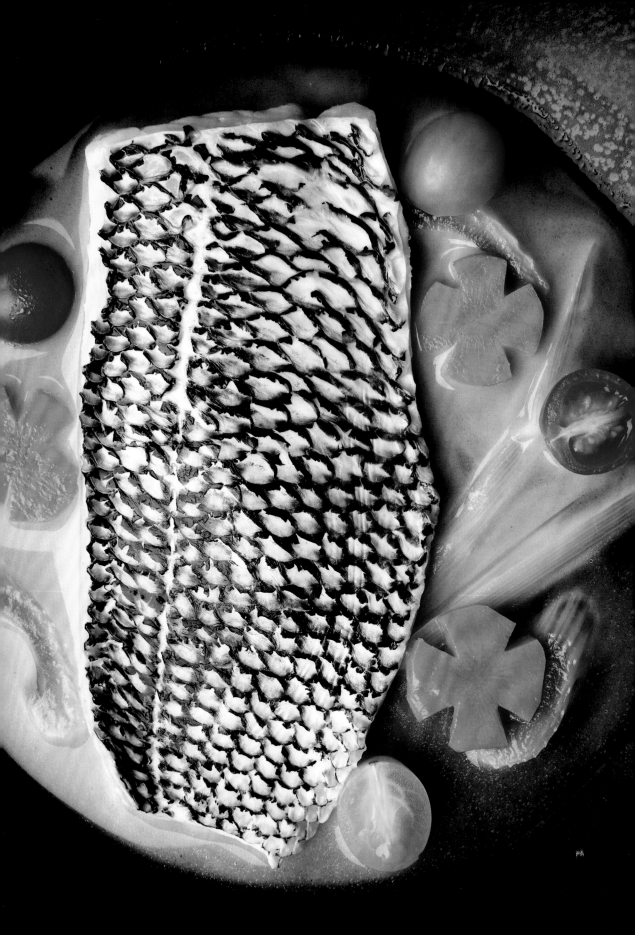

SEAFOOD SIMPLE

Eric Ripert

PHOTOGRAPHS BY NIGEL PARRY

RANDOM HOUSE · NEW YORK

Published in the United States by Random House, an imprint and division
of Penguin Random House LLC, New York.

Random House and the House colophon are registered trademarks
of Penguin Random House LLC.

Hardback ISBN 978-0-5934-4952-3

Ebook ISBN 978-0-5934-4954-7

Printed in China on acid-free paper

randomhousebooks.com

9 8 7 6 5 4 3 2 1

First Edition

Book design by Debbie Glasserman

FOR THE HARD WORK,
PASSION, AND DEDICATION OF THE TEAM
AND THE UNCONDITIONAL LOVE
OF MY FAMILY

CONTENTS

INTRODUCTION

Cooking seafood is, in truth, not that simple. To most cooks, it's a paradox, an oxymoron, an obvious contradiction; a kitchen task perceived as complicated, demanding, and messy. And while it does require a great deal of focus, technical skill, and experience, cooking seafood can be a fun adventure, especially once you start to explore and practice new techniques and recipes. I created this book to remedy these perceptions and to take seafood from daunting to rewarding. Often, home cooks tell me that they are intimidated by preparing fish, that it's overwhelming and they don't know where, or how, to start. You may feel that way, too, and while I completely understand your hesitance, my goal with *Seafood Simple* is to teach you that it really can be just that: simple. I will share with you a series of techniques that are straightforward to master and will help to demystify the process and to guarantee success in your kitchen. My hope is that this book serves as a source of both inspiration and education. The secret to *Seafood Simple* is to trust the process, and yourself!

As a chef whose career of thirty-five years and counting has been committed to seafood, and who is currently at the helm of a restaurant, Le Bernardin, dedicated to seafood, I started writing this cookbook by asking myself: Why now? The truth is, it has taken me decades to truly realize the complexities of seafood, to develop and master a knowledge for it, and to use this understanding and expertise to unpack the misconception that cooking seafood is anything but simple.

My love for eating preceded my love for cooking, which itself preceded my love of fish and seafood. Of course, I wasn't born with knife skills, but my taste buds developed early and furiously. Eating was an utter joy for me, but school on the other hand was not, so enrolling at a small culinary college when I was fifteen was my way of transforming my passion into my career. It was a long journey through culinary school and my first kitchen jobs before I began to understand, learn, and finally master the techniques that today allow me to cook demanding food in complicated ways. But mastering these skills in the kitchen has also taught me a valuable lesson, and one that I hope to impart here: how to strip back the complexities and prepare food that's incredibly simple but just as enjoyable—and often, even more so. (Think about your favorite dish: For many of us, it's something we ate in childhood whose deliciousness lies in how uncomplicated it is. For me, it's a simple fish soup made by Grandma.) This is the most rewarding way to approach cooking: using culinary knowledge to achieve simplicity. This book's nine foundational cooking techniques, which I'll teach you how to master step by step, will show you how working with fish can, indeed, be simple.

By nature, fish is very delicate, in terms of both flavor and texture. When I joined Le Bernardin in 1990, my respect and appreciation for these characteristics deepened under the mentorship of chef Gilbert Le Coze. No one understood fish more than Gilbert, and he wasn't just teaching me the beauty of cooking with seafood, he was educating each and every guest who walked through the doors of the restaurant. Le Bernardin was a pioneer in the style of fish it was serving: prepared simply with few ingredients, like the restaurant's signature dish, Pounded Tuna. Our mantra states that the fish is the star of the plate, and our philosophy of adding only ingredients that elevate and enhance the fish's natural qualities applies even if we're serving a vegetable or a meat dish.

This approach defines our cooking style, and its success lies in the quality of the ingredients we use. It's especially important to source the best quality of produce; if you start with mediocre ingredients, you will have a mediocre result even if you're a genius in the kitchen. It's very difficult to achieve anything good with bad ingredients, and this is especially true when it comes to seafood. There are many variables to consider: Seafood is very sensitive to temperature and time, and (like me) you must be borderline obsessed with how to keep it in the best conditions possible to maintain its freshness. As you cook your way through these recipes, you will notice how obsessive I am about freshness. These reminders serve to highlight just how key freshness is to safe and flavorful seafood. It might sound tricky, but thanks to advances in technology and transport, it is actually easier to source fresh seafood today than ever before. Even as recently as the beginning of the twentieth century, fish was rarely served at restaurants that were beyond close proximity to coasts and local fishermen, and most of the time the fish was smothered in ingredients and heavy sauces to disguise the unmistakable fishy smell and taste of old or bad seafood. Today, at Le Bernardin at least, our sauces and ingredients must complement the fish and celebrate its natural flavors and qualities.

When choosing and sourcing seafood (and everything you cook with), it's important not only to have respect for the ingredients but to practice good ethics and take responsibility for your choices. I have spent a lot of time educating myself over the years about food sourcing, sustainability, and the environmental and economic factors that affect the supply chain. It's essential to know the source of ingredients and to therefore be able to choose the suppliers who engage in good practices for the well-being of the planet. I spend my days with many varieties of fish, considering which are best for the restaurant. This means more than just judging by their flavor and composition. It includes understanding the ethics and politics surrounding how they have been made available to us. While sourcing organic produce is relatively easy, identifying sustainable fish can be more difficult. Some species may be in jeopardy in certain regions but have healthy populations in others, and as the seasons change, so do the lists of species you should be buying. It is worthwhile to do some research to ensure that the fish you're using is not endangered, was fed naturally, and was treated humanely. Several organizations provide information on sea life sustainability, including the Monterey Bay Aquarium Seafood Watch program, the Natural Resources Defense Council (NRDC), Oceana, and the Cousteau Society. In my own research, I also significantly rely on the National Oceanic and Atmospheric Administration (NOAA) to discover where there are overlaps and shared concerns. In America, we are lucky that the U.S. government is proactive in protecting fish species and the coastline, but it's important to educate yourself through research on the current status of seafood species: Take a look at not just which are under pressure or on the verge of disappearing, but also which are abundantly available.

Seafood Simple follows my previous book, *Vegetable Simple*, which was a celebration of vegetables, encouraging cooks to elevate them to main components in our meals. While I see it as a companion book, it's very different in terms of its goals and origins. My intention with *Vegetable Simple* was not to convert you to being a vegetarian or vegan, whereas my intention with *Seafood Simple* is to convert you into a competent and confident seafood cook. If *Vegetable Simple* is a reflection of a new evolution in my eating and cooking habits, *Seafood Simple* is a culmination of the knowledge and expertise I have gained over the course of my career as a professional chef.

The book is broken into chapters organized around what I believe to be the essential, core techniques used to prepare almost any kind of seafood. Within each of the nine techniques is a collection of recipes using specifically selected seafood ingredients that will be best represented by that technique. Of course, there are species of fish that are versatile and can be prepared using more than one technique, such as salmon, which can be raw (poké bowl), steamed (red wine butter), poached (à la Gilbert), slow-baked (olive oil), sautéed (strudel), broiled (carpaccio), and grilled (cedar plank). However, not all techniques are suitable for all fish; for example, poaching is not a good method for meaty or rich fish like tuna but is great for more flaky, lean, and delicate fish like halibut.

You'll find a guide at the back of the book, as well as tips throughout the chapters, to help you navigate aspects of sourcing and shopping, seasonality, sustainability, and storage. While I believe this book to be a sufficient, approachable, and effective road map to seafood success, it is not an exhaustive, in-depth encyclopedia. These recipes and techniques are my topline choices for the quickest and most comprehensive way to achieve the best results. They do not have to be followed in sequence, and I encourage you to begin by trying the ones you find easiest. As with all my cooking, the dishes included in this book were inspired by memorable times in my life: fun experiences while traveling, convivial moments with friends, and celebrations with my family. I truly believe food tastes better when prepared with love, so I hope as this book inspires you to cook with confidence, you will come to approach seafood with joy and, most important, with love.

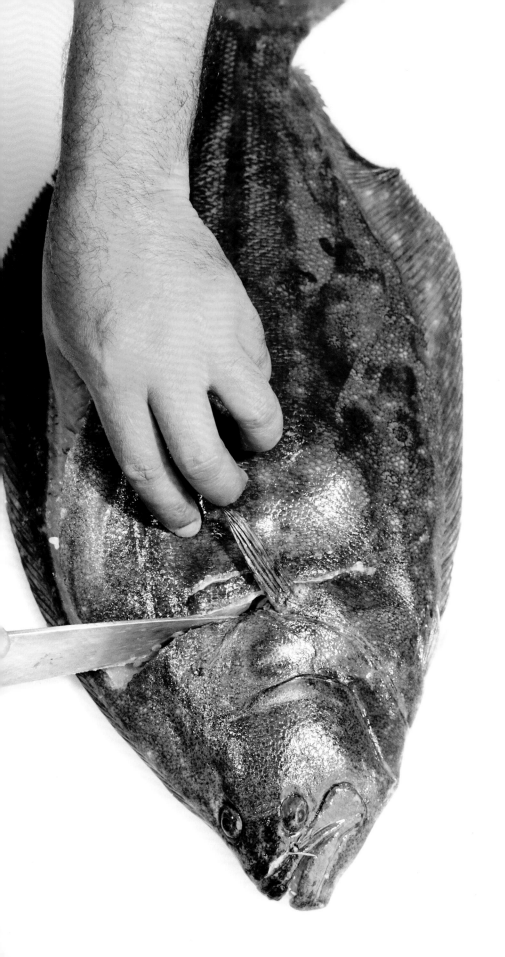

HOW TO FILLET A FLATFISH

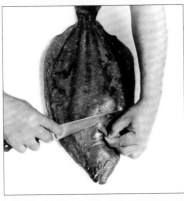  

1. Wash the fish thoroughly to remove any slime, dry it with a towel, and place it on a clean cutting board, with the tail end toward you and the head end (where the organs are) facing away from you.

2. Pull the pectoral fin forward, then make an incision from the fin toward you, following the line between the gills and the head.

3. Insert the tip of the knife at the start of the fillet just over the bones, and, using long strokes, make a shallow cut down the side of the fish.

4. Using the thumb of your nondominant hand, gently lift up the fillet and carefully begin to separate it from the body of the fish using long strokes, cutting just over the bones. Be careful not to cut it all the way through.

5. Cut all the way to the backbone that runs the length of the fish.

5. To release the bottom of the fillet, turn the knife so the sharp end faces the tail. Using the tip of the knife, gently cut over the rib cage, then cut down following the bones. Finally, cut through the skin at the base of the fish to free the fillet from the body of the fish.

6. Turn the fish over with the belly facing you. Pull the pectoral fin toward you and make an incision directly behind the gills from fin to belly.

7. Rotate the fish 180 degrees, then with the tip of the knife, make an incision at the base of the head to expose the backbone. Then proceed to make a shallow cut along the back from head to tail.

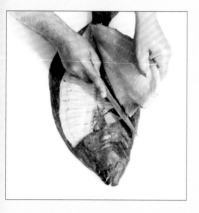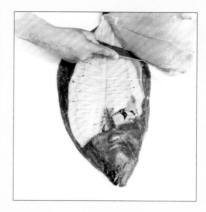

6. Gently cut over the backbone while continuing to lift the fillet away. Finish cutting the fillet away, being careful not to puncture the organs.

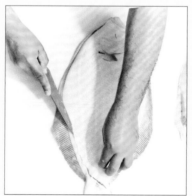

7. Turn the fish over, this time with the head end (and organs) facing you, and repeat the steps on the bottom.

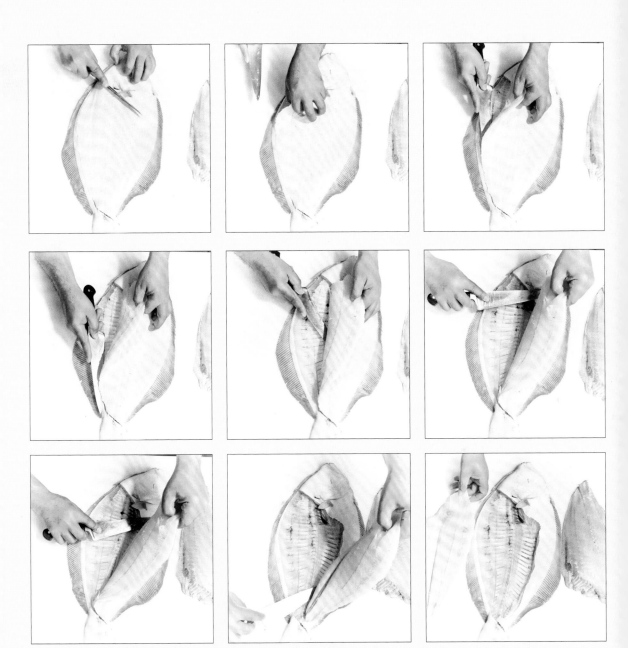

HOW TO FILLET A ROUNDFISH

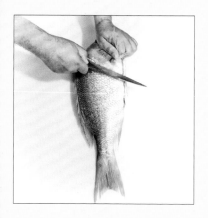  

1. Have the fish scaled, gutted, and rinsed of any innards before filleting.

2. Lay the fish on a cutting board with its back and head facing you. With your free hand, pull the pectoral fin toward you and make a cut directly behind the gills from belly to dorsal fins, making sure not to cut through the backbone.

3. Make a shallow cut at the base of the tail and follow the backbone up the fish and over the dorsal fin to the base of the head.

4. Place the thumb of your nondominant hand under the flesh and pull the fillet up slightly, then, using long strokes, cut horizontally close to the bones to free the top fillet.

8. Place the thumb of your nondominant hand under the flesh, pull up, and, using long strokes, skim the knife over the bones from head to tail to free the top of the fillet.

9. Once the top is released, use the tip of your knife to cut over the rib cage, and then the rest of the fillet from head to tail.

10. Finish by cutting through the skin to free the fillet.

HOW TO SKIN A FISH FILLET

1. For skinning fish, a thin, flexible knife is best.

2. Lay the fillet skin side down on a cutting board, close to the edge of the board. The narrow (tail) end should be facing you.

3. Press firmly on the tail end of the fish with your index finger to anchor it in place. Insert your knife at an angle between the skin and fillet with the blade facing away from you.

4. Grab the skin with your index finger and thumb. Then, using a sawing motion, gently work your knife between the fillet and skin until the knife can lie flat.

5. Grab the skin with your index finger and thumb and gently pull it as you continue to saw with the knife to release the skin from the fillet.

6. Turn the fillet over and make a shallow cut to remove any blood line.

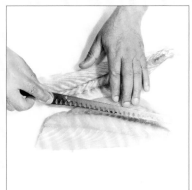

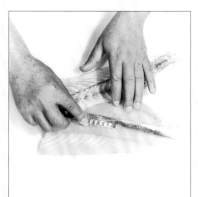

HOW TO CLEAN SHRIMP

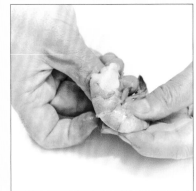

1. Check the shrimp for freshness; the flesh should be firm, shiny, and slightly translucent, with no unpleasant odor.

2. Quickly rinse the shrimp in cold water and drain in a colander.

3. If they are head-on shrimp, first remove the heads: Pinch the shell where the head meets the tail, hold the tail firmly with your other hand, and twist until the tail comes free.

4. Holding the shrimp with the legs facing toward you, place your other thumb at the head end of the shrimp, grab the legs and body, and peel away from you to remove the top portion of the shell.

5. Next, using your thumb and index finger, pinch the tail at the bottom and wiggle the shell off the rest of the meat.

6. Once the shell is removed, using a paring knife, make a small incision along the back ridge of the shrimp, exposing the vein. Using your fingers or the tip of the knife, remove the vein.

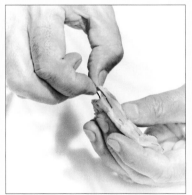  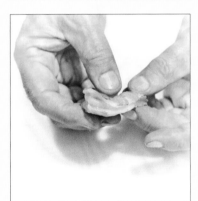

HOW TO SPLIT A LOBSTER

1. Lay the lobster belly down on a cutting board. Place the tip of a sharp knife in the center of the head with the blade pointing toward the front of the head. Press down, splitting the head in two.

2. Carefully remove the rubber band from the lobster's claws with the tip of your knife. Then turn the lobster over and remove the knuckle and claw by twisting them off. Set aside.

3. Return the lobster to the cutting board with its belly side facing up. Starting from where the head meets the tail, cut 90 percent of the way through the body, continuing through the tail. Turn the lobster 180 degrees and continue cutting through the head.

4. Holding the lobster in your hands, open the lobster like a book to expose the flesh and tomalley, the green substance found near the head. Gently wash the head section and remove if not desired.

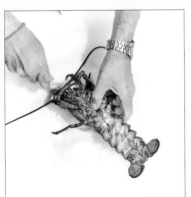  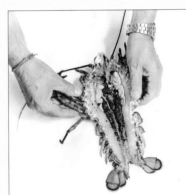

HOW TO SHUCK AN OYSTER

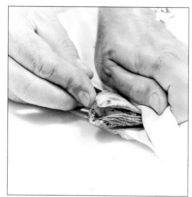

1. Place a kitchen towel on a table in front of you. Fold the towel in half lengthwise and then in half again, giving you a pocket to hold the oyster.

2. Place an oyster, belly side (rounded side) down, in the fold with the hinge of the oyster (the pointed back end) facing out.

3. Using your nondominant hand, firmly put pressure on top of the towel to hold the oyster in place.

4. With your dominant hand, place the tip of an oyster knife into the oyster's hinge and slowly wiggle the knife to find the separation point to break the ligament that keeps the two shells together. You will feel a small pop when the shells detach.

5. Once the shell is detached, twist the knife so that the handle now points toward you and slide the tip of the knife under the top side of the shell. This will detach the adductor muscle so you can remove the top shell.

6. Gently slide the tip of the knife underneath the oyster to detach the adductor muscle from the bottom shell, while keeping the oyster sitting inside the bottom shell. Check for pieces of shell or debris and remove them. Smell the oyster for freshness and discard any oyster that smells off.

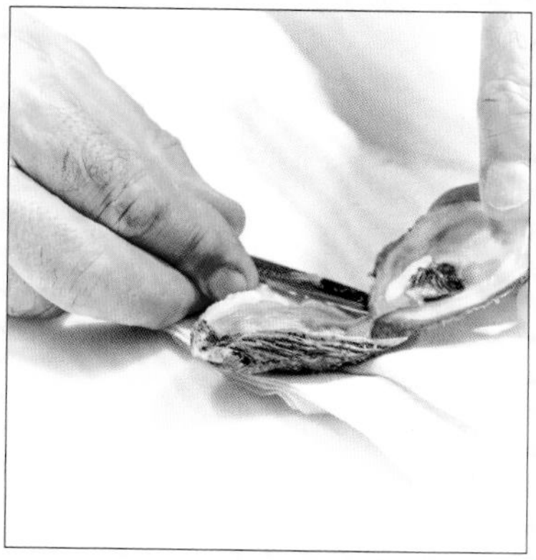

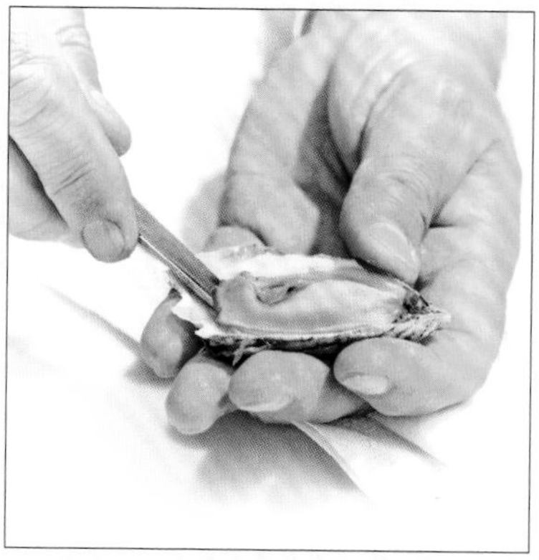

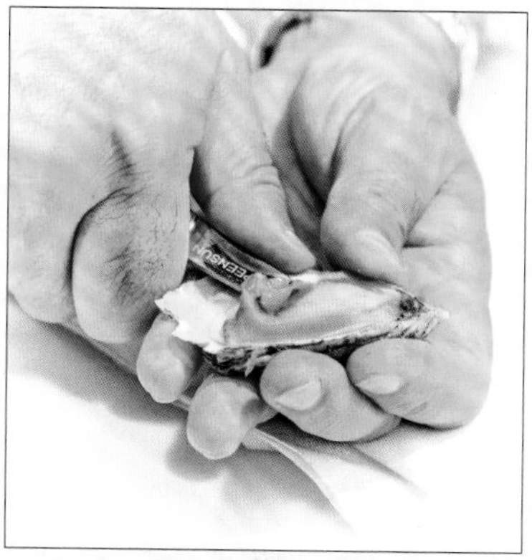

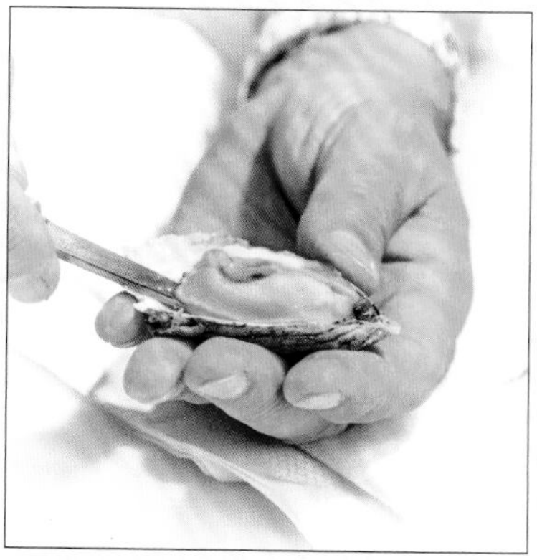

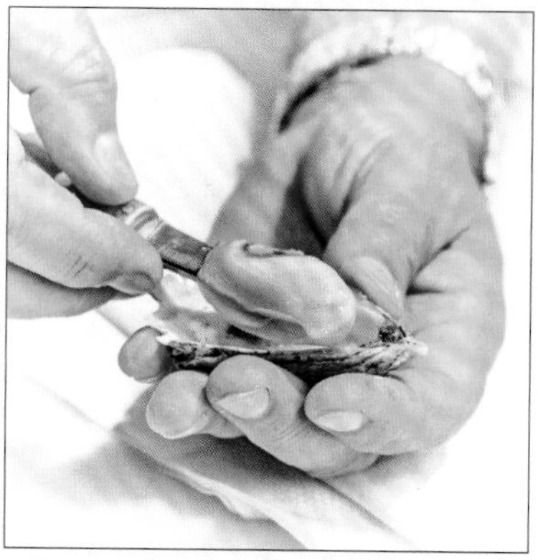

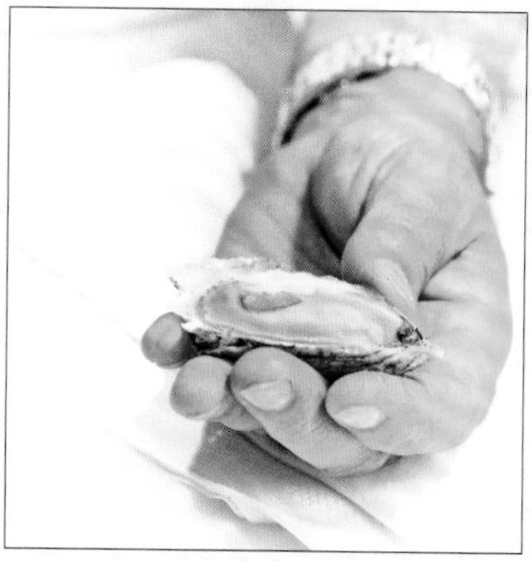

HOW TO SHUCK A CLAM

1. Wash the clams thoroughly in cold water.

2. Keep the clams cold, either on a tray lying flat in the refrigerator or on ice.

3. Using a towel or glove (not pictured), hold a clam in your nondominant hand with the hinge tucked in toward your palm where it meets the thumb.

4. Insert the tip of a clam knife or paring knife between the top and bottom shells. Cut around the front lip of the clam, between the two halves of the shell, then twist to pry it open.

5. With the tip of the knife, disconnect the clam meat from the top shell.

6. Twist off the top shell, then, with the tip of the knife, disconnect the meat from the bottom shell.

HOW TO REMOVE PIN BONES

1. Lay the fish on a cutting board skin side down.

2. Run the side of your finger over the fish, feeling for little bones that run in a line near the center of the fish.

3. Using needle-nose pliers or fish tweezers, firmly grip each pin bone, pulling down and away.

4. Continue removing pin bones one by one. Gently pass your hand over the flesh to check for any missed bones.

HOW TO SEASON

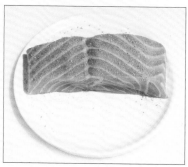

To properly season something, make sure you are working with clean, dry hands. Evenly sprinkle salt and pepper on both sides of foods from about 6 inches away using steady sweeping motions over the food. Always remember to taste the food and adjust the seasoning as needed throughout cooking.

1

RAW, CURED & MARINATED

RAW

Uncooked

CURE

To preserve food by one of several methods, including with salt, smoke, or pickle brine

MARINATE

To cover food (seafood, meat, vegetables) in a seasoned / flavored liquid, usually combining vinegar, wine, or another acidic liquid with oil, herbs, and spices

There are many different species of fish that can be served raw or are suitable to be cured; however, not all raw and cured seafood should be treated the same. For instance, an oyster (a bivalve) would be treated differently from a meaty fish like tuna, which would be treated differently from a leaner fish like fluke.

But what all seafood should have in common when being served raw or cured is freshness: You should work with the freshest fish possible, for reasons of both safety and flavor. For example, oysters and clams are freshest and best when still alive, just before opening. Seafood takes on that telltale "fishy" smell and flavor the longer it is out of water. To ensure you are serving your fish as fresh as it can be after you've purchased it, you need to work fast and work clean. Fish should always be kept cold; it should never sit at room temperature for long.

If you are serving seafood raw, the easiest way to enhance its qualities and draw out its flavor is to add acidity, like fresh lemon or lime juice. If the acidity is too strong, you can tame it by adding a little olive oil to balance it out. There are several different methods and styles of preparing raw seafood, including crudo, where the fish is cut thick sashimi-style, and carpaccio, where the fish is sliced and pounded very thinly. Most raw seafood dishes are served as appetizers; this group of recipes is a shortlist of some of my favorite, as well as the simplest raw and cured appetizers and small plates.

CARPACCIO TECHNIQUE

1. Cover a work surface, such as a counter or table, with a large sheet of plastic wrap. Place one 4-ounce piece of fish in the center and cover it with another large sheet of plastic.

2. Flatten the fish with a meat pounder (or a heavy-bottomed saucepan), using a fluid motion that combines hitting the fish in the center and sliding the surface of the pounder over the fish, pressing it outward. Continue pounding and pressing out the fish until it forms a very thin, even round, about 9 inches in diameter.

3. Place an 8-inch round plate, bowl, or cake pan to use as a cutting guide over the fish (still keeping the fish covered with plastic) and use a sharp knife to cut through the fish and both layers of plastic, resulting in an 8-inch round. Leave the plastic on until ready to serve. Repeat with each portion of fish. Refrigerate for at least 30 minutes before serving.

4. When ready to serve, pull the top plastic sheet off one tuna round and place the tuna on the center of a large dinner plate, plastic side up. Remove the plastic from the top of the tuna. Repeat with the remaining 3 tuna rounds.

  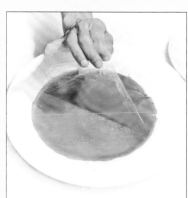

OYSTERS MIGNONETTE

MIGNONETTE

¼ cup red wine vinegar

Fine sea salt

2 tablespoons finely chopped shallot

½ teaspoon freshly ground black pepper

OYSTERS

12 very fresh oysters

Lemon juice

Extra-virgin olive oil

SPECIAL EQUIPMENT

Oyster knife

When it comes to oysters, freshness is tantamount to quality. As a general rule, the best months to enjoy oysters are those containing the letter "r"—September through April. During the summer months, oysters are spawning, and the temperatures are too warm for them to reach their optimum quality.

The ultimate test of an oyster's freshness is to smell it. It should not have a strong, pungent odor. Then, take a look at it: The oyster should be clean and have a nice weight to it, which tells you there's still salt water inside—if the oyster is too light, that means it has lost its body water, which makes it die quickly and become dry and chewy. Oysters are best eaten when they are alive, which you can test by opening the oyster and touching its mantle (the fine layer of tissue around its body) with the blade of a knife. If the oyster retracts, it's still alive. You can also test this with a drop of lemon juice.

For beginners, I recommend starting with small to medium oysters and sourcing them no more than 24 hours before you plan to serve. Refrigerate them immediately in an open-top plastic or glass container with the oysters stacked on top of one another, rounded belly side down, flat side up—this prevents them from opening and losing their liquid.

1. Make the mignonette: In a bowl, combine the vinegar and a pinch of sea salt. Stir to dissolve. Stir in the shallot and black pepper.

2. Shuck the oysters (see photos, pages 14 and 15): Place a kitchen towel on a table in front of you. Fold the towel in half lengthwise, then in half again, giving you a pocket to hold the oyster.

3. Place an oyster, belly side (rounded side) down, in the fold with the hinge of the oyster (the pointed back end) facing out.

Recipe continues

4. Using your nondominant hand, firmly put pressure on top of the towel to hold the oyster in place.

5. With your dominant hand, place the tip of an oyster knife into the oyster's hinge and slowly wiggle the knife to find the separation point to break the ligament that keeps the two shells together. You will feel a small pop when the shells detach.

6. Once the shell is detached, twist the knife so that the handle now points toward you and slide the tip of the knife under the top side of the shell. This will detach the adductor muscle so you can remove the top shell.

7. Gently slide the tip of the knife underneath the oyster to detach the adductor muscle from the bottom shell, while keeping the oyster sitting inside the bottom shell. Check for pieces of shell or debris and remove them. Smell the oyster for freshness and discard any oyster that smells off.

8. Place the oysters over crushed ice.

9. Spoon mignonette over 6 of the oysters.

10. For the remaining oysters, add a squeeze of fresh lemon juice and a splash of extra-virgin olive oil to each. Serve immediately.

GRAVLAX, BLINIS, AND CAVIAR

SERVES 6 TO 8

While gravlax takes a few days to cure, it is easy to make and so rewarding when it's ready to eat—definitely worth the wait. Use the freshest salmon you can get your hands on. I recommend buying good-quality, farm-raised salmon (wild can often have too little fat for this preparation).

When shopping for the roe or caviar, don't be shy about asking the store representative to open the tin so you can look, smell, and taste the product. Roes have bright flavors and should never be oily or too salty, or have a muddy after-taste.

1. Make the gravlax: In a small bowl, mix together the brown sugar, salt, and pepper.

2. Line a work surface with a large piece of plastic wrap. Set both pieces of salmon on the plastic wrap and rub three-quarters of the salt and sugar mixture all over each piece. Cover the flesh sides with half the chopped dill, then splash with the vodka or gin.

3. Place the salmon fillets together like a sandwich, skin sides out, and rub with the remaining salt and sugar mixture and dill. Enclose the fish in the plastic wrap, set in a baking dish, and refrigerate.

4. Every 12 to 14 hours, open the package and baste with the juices that have come out. The fish is ready when the flesh is opaque, usually by the second or third day.

5. Once the gravlax is cured, make the blinis: In a saucepan or in the microwave, bring the milk to 105°F. In a small bowl, dissolve the yeast in ½ cup of the warm milk, then stir in the sugar. Cover with plastic wrap and keep warm until foamy, 10 to 15 minutes.

6. Meanwhile, in a large bowl, combine the flour and sea salt.

GRAVLAX

1 cup packed light brown sugar

½ cup Diamond Crystal kosher salt

1½ teaspoons freshly ground black pepper

2- to 3-pound salmon fillet, skin on, pin bones removed, halved crosswise through the center to form 2 equal pieces

1 bunch fresh dill, chopped

3 tablespoons vodka or gin

BLINIS

3½ cups whole milk

1 envelope (2¼ teaspoons) active dry yeast

2 teaspoons sugar

4 cups all-purpose flour

1 teaspoon fine sea salt

2 large eggs, at room temperature

2 tablespoons canola oil or melted butter

Additional canola oil or cooking spray for cooking

GARNISHES

Caviar

Smoked trout roe

Crème fraîche (optional)

Recipe continues

RAW, CURED & MARINATED

7. In a separate bowl, whisk together the eggs and canola oil. Add the foamy yeast mixture and the remaining 3 cups lukewarm milk. Mix well to combine.

8. Slowly add the milk mixture to the flour mixture and whisk well to combine. Cover with plastic wrap and let rise in a warm place for 2 to 3 hours, stirring once every hour. The batter should have the consistency of a thick milkshake.

9. To cook the blinis, heat a nonstick, cast-iron, or blini pan lightly coated with canola oil or cooking spray over medium heat. Stir the batter. Working in batches, spoon 1 to 2 tablespoons of batter into the pan, forming as many blinis as will fit without touching. When the blinis begin to rise and bubble in the center, carefully flip with an offset spatula and cook until golden brown, about 2 minutes. Transfer the blinis to a plate as they finish cooking. Repeat with the remaining batter, stirring before each use. Add more oil to the pan as needed.

10. Rinse the salmon to remove any remaining salt and pat dry. Holding your knife at a 45-degree angle to the cutting board, thinly slice the salmon on a bias, leaving the skin behind.

11. Serve the blinis with the gravlax, caviar, smoked trout roe, and, if desired, crème fraîche.

YELLOWTAIL (HAMACHI) CRUDO

SERVES 4

12 ounces yellowtail (hamachi) loin, skinned and blood line removed

Fine sea salt

1 Meyer lemon, for zesting

Freshly ground black pepper

Maldon salt

Extra-virgin olive oil

This westernized version of sashimi is one of my favorite ways to showcase fresh hamachi (yellowtail). I like to serve this with toast, which creates a wonderful contrast between the soft texture of the fish and the crunch of the bread.

The freshness of the hamachi is paramount here; as there are so few ingredients, the fish should have nothing to hide behind! The flesh of this fish should be slightly translucent and vibrant, not opaque or beige or showing any dullness. The usual smell test applies (this fish should have zero smell), but your eyes will also tell you a lot about the level of freshness. If you do see blood lines, they should be bright red, never dark red, and make sure to remove them during prep.

1. Make sure the fish is cold and your knife is sharp. Holding the knife at a 45-degree angle to the cutting board, slice the yellowtail into about twenty ¼-inch-thick slices.

2. Lightly season the yellowtail with sea salt and transfer 5 slices to each plate, slightly overlapping the slices.

3. Using a Microplane or zester, grate the zest of the Meyer lemon directly over the fish. Finish with black pepper, a few flakes of Maldon salt, and a generous splash of good extra-virgin olive oil. Serve immediately.

TUNA CARPACCIO

SERVES 4

There are many different species of tuna available, including bluefin, bigeye, and yellowfin. The latter is best suited for a great carpaccio, whereas bluefin and bigeye tuna are better for cooking or for serving in bigger, thicker pieces. The texture of yellowfin tuna lends itself well to carpaccio because its lower fat content prevents it from becoming mushy, thus helping it keep its firmness during the pounding process. The tuna shouldn't be too dark, but it shouldn't have an unnaturally bright color, either. You should be looking for yellowfin with a hue between light pinkish and soft orange, with brown being an absolute no-no. Tuna that's too red should also be avoided as that means there is too much blood, which, when served raw, will give it an unpleasant taste.

Once you start to dress this dish, go very fast and serve it immediately, as the acidity of the lemon juice starts to cook the fish and change the flavor of the tuna.

4 pieces (4 ounces each) sushi-quality yellowfin tuna, cut ½ inch thick

Fine sea salt and freshly ground white pepper

4 tablespoons extra-virgin olive oil

2 teaspoons thinly sliced fresh chives

1 lemon, halved and seeded

Toasted baguette slices for serving

SPECIAL EQUIPMENT

Flat meat pounder

Wide pastry brush

1. Cover a work surface, such as a counter or table, with a large sheet of plastic wrap. Place 1 piece of tuna in the center and cover it with another large sheet of plastic. (See photos, pages 24 and 25.)

2. Flatten the tuna with a meat pounder (or a heavy-bottomed saucepan), using a fluid motion that combines hitting the tuna in the center and sliding the surface of the pounder over the fish, pressing it outward. Continue pounding and pressing out the tuna until it forms a very thin, even round, about 9 inches in diameter.

3. Place an 8-inch round plate, bowl, or cake pan to use as a cutting guide over the tuna (still keeping the fish covered with plastic) and use a sharp knife to cut through the tuna and both layers of plastic, resulting in an 8-inch round. Leave the plastic on the tuna and transfer to a sheet pan. Repeat with each portion of tuna. Refrigerate for

Recipe continues

30 minutes. (The tuna can be pounded and cut up to a few hours ahead; cover the entire tray with plastic and refrigerate.)

4. When ready to serve, pull the top plastic sheet off one tuna round and place the tuna on the center of a large dinner plate, plastic side up. Remove the plastic from the top of the tuna. Repeat with the remaining 3 tuna rounds.

5. Season each round with sea salt and white pepper. Dip a wide pastry brush in the olive oil and coat each piece of tuna generously with oil. Sprinkle each portion with the chives, then squeeze lemon juice over the top. Wipe the edge of each plate with a towel. Serve immediately, with the toasted baguette slices on a separate plate alongside.

TUNA CARPACCIO
WITH GINGER-LIME MAYONNAISE
SERVES 4

Carpaccio should have an even thickness, ideally ⅛ inch but no less than 1/16 inch—this might sound nerdy and overly precise, but it is key to achieving the right texture. If too thin, the tuna will have no texture, and if too thick, it will be chewy.

1. Cover a work surface, such as a counter or table, with a large sheet of plastic wrap. Place 1 piece of tuna in the center and cover it with another large sheet of plastic. (See photos, pages 24 and 25.)

2. Flatten the tuna with a meat pounder (or a heavy-bottomed saucepan), using a fluid motion that combines hitting the tuna in the center and sliding the surface of the pounder over the fish, pressing it outward. Continue pounding and pressing out the tuna until it forms a very thin, even round, about 9 inches in diameter.

3. Place an 8-inch round plate, bowl, or cake pan to use as a cutting guide over the tuna (still keeping the fish covered with plastic) and use a sharp knife to cut through the tuna and both layers of plastic, resulting in an 8-inch round. Leave the plastic on the tuna and transfer to a sheet pan. Repeat with each portion of tuna. Refrigerate for 30 minutes. (The tuna can be pounded and cut up to a few hours ahead; cover the entire tray with plastic and refrigerate.)

4. Make the ginger-lime mayonnaise: In a small bowl, combine the mayonnaise, ginger juice, and lime juice and whisk until smooth. Season with a pinch of sea salt.

5. When ready to serve, pull the top plastic sheet off one tuna round and place the tuna on the center of a large dinner plate, plastic side up. Remove the plastic from the top of the tuna. Repeat with the remaining 3 tuna rounds.

6. Season with sea salt and white pepper. Using the side of a pastry brush, paint a thin layer of mayonnaise onto the tuna, starting at the center and moving toward the edge, then curving back to the center like a flower petal.

7. To finish, put a small mound of mâche in the center of each plate and lightly drizzle the greens with olive oil. Serve immediately.

4 pieces (4 ounces each) sushi-quality yellowfin tuna, cut ½ inch thick

GINGER-LIME MAYONNAISE

¼ cup mayonnaise

1 tablespoon Ginger Juice (page 39)

1 tablespoon fresh lime juice

Fine sea salt

FOR SERVING

Fine sea salt and freshly ground white pepper

1 cup mâche

Extra-virgin olive oil

SPECIAL EQUIPMENT

Flat meat pounder

Wide pastry brush

Recipe continues

GINGER JUICE

MAKES 2 TO 3 TABLESPOONS

1. Peel the ginger, then line a small bowl with cheesecloth.

2. Using a Microplane or fine grater, grate the ginger into the cheesecloth.

3. Wrap the grated ginger in the cloth and squeeze over the bowl to release the juice, then transfer it to a sealed container and refrigerate until ready to use.

3-inch piece fresh ginger

SPECIAL EQUIPMENT

Cheesecloth

SNAPPER CARPACCIO

SERVES 4

4 (6-inch-long) snapper fillets, skinned

Fine sea salt and freshly ground white pepper

¼ cup extra-virgin olive oil

8 multicolored cherry tomatoes, cut into ⅛-inch-thick rounds (about 32 rounds)

16 thin slices jalapeño pepper

28 small fresh basil leaves

1 lemon, halved and seeded

SPECIAL EQUIPMENT

Flat meat pounder

Wide pastry brush

At the risk of repeating myself throughout the book, I cannot overstate the importance of freshness when it comes to fish—*fresh* and *fish* go hand in hand, but even more so when you're planning to serve it raw.

Snapper has a luminous, almost glassy flesh. After slicing the fish, you may notice it has some white strings attached to the flesh throughout—these are nerves and should be removed delicately. Any blood lines should also be removed before making the carpaccio. You can prepare the carpaccio portion of this dish earlier in the day, but it should not sit for more than 12 hours. Store in the coldest section of the refrigerator and garnish at the very last minute. Timing is essential for this preparation, so I recommend that you first make this dish for two people so as not to overwhelm yourself or rush the process; when you become more comfortable with it, increase the serving to four people and so on.

1. Using a very sharp knife, cut each snapper fillet lengthwise into ¼-inch-wide strips, keeping the slices in order.

2. Cover a work surface, such as a counter or table, with a large sheet of plastic wrap. Gently place the snapper strips from one fillet in the center, leaving a small gap between the slices. Cover with another sheet of plastic wrap and firmly press down.

3. Flatten the fish with a meat pounder (or a heavy-bottomed saucepan), using a fluid motion that combines hitting the fish in the center and sliding the surface of the pounder over the fish, pressing it outward. Continue pounding and pressing out the fish until it forms a very thin, even round, about 9 inches in diameter. (See photos, pages 24 and 25.)

4. Place an 8-inch round plate, bowl, or cake pan to use as a cutting guide over the fish (still keeping the fish covered with plastic) and use a sharp knife to cut through the fish and both layers of plastic, resulting in an 8-inch round. Leave the plastic on the fish and transfer to a sheet pan. Repeat with each portion of fish. Refrigerate for 30 minutes. (The snapper can be pounded and cut up to a few hours ahead; cover the entire tray with plastic and refrigerate.)

5. When ready to serve, pull the top plastic sheet off one snapper round and place the fish on the center of a large dinner plate, plastic side up. Remove the plastic from the top of the snapper. Repeat with the remaining 3 snapper rounds.

6. Season the snapper with sea salt and white pepper. Using a pastry brush, gently coat the top of each round with olive oil. Divide the tomatoes, jalapeño, and basil evenly over the snapper and finish with a squeeze of lemon juice. Serve immediately.

BLACK BASS TARTARE

SERVES 4

A sharp knife, patience, and precision are your friends when making tartare. Dicing the bass in small, even pieces is a key part of the dish's aesthetic appeal. Evenly distribute the dice on the plate to ensure balanced seasoning, and make sure to chill the tartare before garnishing. You can plate this dish up to an hour before serving. However, do wait until the last moment to add the salt, lemon, and olive oil; if you add the olive oil too soon, the dish will lose its textural contrast.

¾ pound black bass fillets, skinned and cut into ¼-inch dice

½ tomato, seeded and cut into ⅛-inch dice

2 tablespoons fresh basil chiffonade

2 teaspoons drained baby capers

Fine sea salt and freshly ground white pepper

6 tablespoons extra-virgin olive oil

1 lemon, halved and seeded

1. Divide the black bass evenly among four chilled plates, using a fork to gently spread the bass into a flat, even layer that covers most of the plate. Cover each plate with plastic wrap and refrigerate until ready to serve, up to a few hours.

2. When ready to serve, evenly sprinkle the tomatoes, basil, and capers over the fish and season lightly with sea salt and white pepper. Drizzle 1½ tablespoons olive oil over each serving, then add a generous squeeze of lemon juice. Taste and adjust seasoning if necessary, and serve immediately.

RAW, CURED & MARINATED

SPANISH MACKEREL TARTARE
WITH CAVIAR
SERVES 4

TARTARE

¾ pound Spanish mackerel fillets, skinned and blood line removed, cut into ¼-inch dice

Fine sea salt and freshly ground white pepper

2 ounces osetra caviar

1 tablespoon fresh lemon juice

2 teaspoons canola oil

2 teaspoons thinly sliced fresh chives

SAUCE

¼ cup crème fraîche

2 teaspoons vodka

1 teaspoon freshly ground black pepper

Fine sea salt

FOR SERVING

8 slices Melba toast

SPECIAL EQUIPMENT

Four 3-inch ring molds

Mackerel is rich and fatty, so in order to slice the fish cleanly, you must keep it extremely cold. Work fast and carefully in the coolest area of your kitchen or prep space. For prepping the mackerel, I recommend taking it from the fridge and dicing it in small batches, returning each batch to the fridge when done.

Here we're using golden osetra caviar—which is lighter in color than other roes, with slightly honey-toned pearls—but this dish works excellently with a darker caviar as well. The mackerel portion can be prepped ahead of time; make sure you leave enough room in the ring mold to top with the caviar just before serving.

1. Make the tartare: Place the diced mackerel in a bowl and season lightly with sea salt and white pepper. Stir in 1 tablespoon of the caviar along with the lemon juice, canola oil, and chives. Taste and adjust seasoning if necessary. Refrigerate until needed, up to 3 or 4 hours.

2. Make the sauce: Fill a large bowl halfway with ice cubes and set a smaller bowl on top of the ice. Put the crème fraîche in the smaller bowl and whisk until soft peaks form. Add the vodka and continue to whisk until the peaks re-form. Add the black pepper and whisk to combine. Season lightly with sea salt. Taste and adjust seasoning if necessary. Refrigerate until ready to use.

3. To serve, place a 3-inch ring mold in the center of a chilled plate and spoon in one-quarter of the tartare. Top with one-quarter of the remaining caviar and remove the ring mold. Repeat with the remaining ingredients and three more plates.

4. Gently spoon 1 tablespoon of the crème fraîche/vodka sauce onto each plate and serve immediately with Melba toasts alongside.

SCALLOP CEVICHE

SERVES 4

Live scallops will make the very best version of this dish. If you are lucky enough to source live ones in the shell (tap the scallop gently; if the shell closes, the scallop is still alive) and you know how to open and clean them, their quality and firmness is unmatchable. But don't let this deter you from attempting this dish—you can find good, fresh scallops at fishmongers and good grocery stores that will work perfectly well. Scallops should be firm and fairly translucent, not very white or too opaque in color, nor too soft in texture. Serving the scallop in the shell is aesthetically pleasing but not necessary. Prepare just before you plan to serve.

8 diver scallops, cut into ½-inch dice

Fine sea salt and freshly ground white pepper

2 teaspoons fresh lemon juice

¼ cup extra-virgin olive oil

2 tablespoons minced fresh chives

Espelette pepper (optional)

1. Place the scallops in a bowl and season with sea salt and white pepper. Add the lemon juice and stir to combine. Stir in the olive oil to coat, followed by the chives. Taste and adjust seasoning if necessary.

2. To serve, place a small mound of ceviche in the center of four plates or scallop shells. If you like spice, add a pinch of Espelette pepper. Serve immediately.

FLUKE CEVICHE

SERVES 6

1½ pounds fluke fillet, skinned

¾ cup fresh lime juice (about 4 juicy limes)

¼ cup thinly sliced red onion

Fine sea salt and freshly ground white pepper

2 tablespoons roughly chopped fresh cilantro

2 teaspoons roughly chopped fresh mint

2 teaspoons fresh basil chiffonade

1 teaspoon minced jalapeño pepper

For this dish, I was inspired by the traditional Peruvian way of making ceviche, and particularly by ceviche master Javier Wong of Chez Wong in Lima, Peru. He makes ceviche at the speed of light, from filleting the fish to plating in mere minutes. Fluke is a very tender fish with a lot of sweetness. Cutting it into cubes or large pieces and marinating in lime helps release the fluke's own juice, known as *leche de tigre* ("tiger's milk"), which, according to some anecdotes, contains hangover-curing qualities—take that information how you will! In keeping with tradition, this ceviche is rustic in style and presentation. In terms of flavor, it's robust and full of vibrancy, with emphasis on the unique juice that is powerful and delicate all at once.

1. Cut the fluke into 1-inch pieces and place them in a bowl. Cover and refrigerate.

2. Strain the lime juice through a fine-mesh sieve into a separate bowl. Add the red onion and season with sea salt and white pepper.

3. Generously season the fluke with sea salt and white pepper. Add the lime juice and red onion mixture along with the cilantro, mint, basil, and jalapeño. Gently toss to combine. Let the fluke marinate for 5 minutes to allow the juices to be extracted from the fish.

4. Divide the ceviche evenly among six small bowls and serve immediately.

TUNA TARTARE

SERVES 4

Cut the tuna no sooner than the day you are planning to serve, and if you are not preparing the fish right away, keep it refrigerated with plastic wrap pressed tightly against the flesh to prevent it from oxidizing and losing its beautiful color. The ingredients should be mixed just prior to plating so that no one flavor overwhelms the dish. If you can't find fresh ginger, you can substitute powdered ginger, but use it sparingly—usually half the amount of fresh ginger—as it is more concentrated. Be careful not to overmix, as this not only tends to make the fish mushy but also lets more air in, which increases the oxidization process.

1 pound sushi-quality yellowfin tuna

Fine sea salt and freshly ground white pepper

1 tablespoon canola oil

2 teaspoons wasabi paste

1½ teaspoons grated fresh ginger

1 tablespoon thinly sliced fresh chives

Store-bought puffed corn or puffed lentil chips

SPECIAL EQUIPMENT

Four 3-inch ring molds

1. Trim off and discard any blood line. Cut the tuna into ¼-inch dice.

2. Place the tuna in a bowl and lightly season it with sea salt and white pepper.

3. In a small bowl, stir together the oil, wasabi, and ginger until smooth. Using chopsticks or a fork, gently stir the wasabi mixture into the tuna. Add the chives and stir again to combine. Taste and adjust seasoning if necessary.

4. Place a 3-inch ring mold in the center of a bowl and fill with one-quarter of the tartare. Repeat with the remaining tartare and three more bowls. Remove the ring molds, garnish with puffed chips on top, and serve right away.

SALMON POKÉ

SERVES 4

SALMON POKÉ

¼ cup good-quality soy sauce

Pinch of sugar

1¼ pounds salmon fillet, skinned and pin bones removed, cut into ¾-inch dice

1 avocado, cubed

¼ cup thinly sliced quartered red onion

¼ cup thinly sliced scallion

2 tablespoons furikake seasoning

1 tablespoon fresh lime juice

1 teaspoon grated fresh ginger

½ teaspoon toasted sesame oil

STEAMED RICE

1 cup jasmine rice

1 teaspoon fine sea salt

FOR SERVING

2 tablespoons chopped fresh cilantro

Pinch of red pepper flakes

Inspired by Hawaiian poké culture, this dish uses salmon, but you can substitute tuna, which is traditional for poké, if you prefer. Keep the rice warm, even a little bit hot, and top with the cold salmon and garnishes at the last minute to achieve a delicious contrast between temperatures and textures.

1. Prepare the salmon: In a small bowl, combine the soy sauce, sugar, and 1 teaspoon water and stir to dissolve the sugar.

2. Add the salmon, avocado, onion, scallion, furikake, lime juice, ginger, and sesame oil. Mix well, cover, and refrigerate for at least 1 hour and up to overnight.

3. Make the rice: Place the rice in a bowl and cover with cold water. Let stand for 5 minutes, then drain in a fine-mesh sieve. Rinse the rice until the water runs clear.

4. In a medium saucepan, bring 1½ cups water to a boil. Stir in the rice and sea salt, return to a simmer, cover, reduce the heat to low, and simmer for 15 minutes. Remove from the heat and let the rice steam, covered, for 5 minutes. Uncover and fluff the rice. Set aside and keep warm.

5. When ready to serve, divide the jasmine rice among four bowls. Add the cilantro and pepper flakes to the salmon and toss gently. Top the bowls of rice with the salmon mixture, dividing it evenly, and serve immediately.

CRAB SALAD
WITH GAZPACHO SAUCE
SERVES 6

This recipe calls for peekytoe crab from Maine, but you can use any type of crab you can find locally. Just be sure to check for cartilage or shells; be diligent but also delicate when removing any fragments, as you don't want to break up the meat too much. If you don't want to go through this process, you can find good-quality packaged and shelled crabmeat in grocery stores, but don't forget the smell test—crab should have a sweet and pleasant shellfish smell, not overly strong or fishy. I like to combine the crab with the mayonnaise a few hours in advance of serving to enhance their complementary flavors.

1. In a blender, combine the red tomatoes and olive oil and pulse until just pureed. Pass the puree through a fine-mesh sieve into a bowl, pushing a spatula against the solids to extract as much tomato pulp as possible. Add the vinegar to the puree, stir, and season to taste with sea salt and white pepper. Cover and refrigerate.

2. Peel the green tomatoes with a vegetable peeler. Core them, halve them crosswise, and scoop out any seeds. Cut them into batons. Transfer to a bowl and add the lemon oil. Season to taste with sea salt and white pepper. Cover and refrigerate until ready to serve.

3. In a large bowl, combine the sherry vinaigrette and mayonnaise and whisk until smooth. Add the crabmeat and chives and gently stir to combine. Season to taste with sea salt and white pepper. Cover and refrigerate until ready to serve.

4. To serve, place a 4-inch ring mold just left of center in each of six wide, shallow bowls. Divide the crab mixture evenly among the molds. Top each with green tomato salad. Spoon the gazpacho sauce around the mold on each plate. Remove the ring molds and serve immediately.

3 large red tomatoes, cored, seeded, and roughly chopped

3 tablespoons extra-virgin olive oil

2 tablespoons sherry vinegar

Fine sea salt and freshly ground white pepper

2 green tomatoes

3 tablespoons lemon-infused olive oil

3 tablespoons Sherry Vinaigrette (page 56)

3 tablespoons mayonnaise

12 ounces lump peekytoe crabmeat, picked over to remove bits of shell and cartilage

2 tablespoons thinly sliced fresh chives

SPECIAL EQUIPMENT

Six 4-inch ring molds

Recipe continues

SHERRY VINAIGRETTE

3 tablespoons sherry vinegar

1 teaspoon Dijon mustard

½ teaspoon fine sea salt

Pinch of white pepper

½ cup extra-virgin olive oil

In a small bowl, whisk together the vinegar, mustard, sea salt, and white pepper until the salt dissolves. Constantly whisking, slowly drizzle in the olive oil. Store remaining vinaigrette in an airtight container in the refrigerator for up to three days.

2 STEAMED

STEAM

To cook with steam from boiling water

There are many benefits to cooking with steam. It's a softer, lighter way to prepare seafood, as its indirect heat is more gentle than boiling fish in water. While it can be slower than other cooking processes, it yields very tender results and cooks seafood very evenly. Just make sure to be attentive to the timing, since the outside of the flesh can become dry if left to steam for too long.

This is a particularly good way to cook mussels, clams, and other shellfish from the bivalve family, as they steam in their own juices. When their shells open with help from the steam, the shellfish release their juices and cook quickly with some added aromatics, making for a simple, delicious meal. I also like to steam fish by first wrapping it in a banana leaf, collard greens, or parchment paper or foil (en papillote), which seals in the flavors. Dumplings are another great vessel for seafood, and are best steamed in order to maintain the soft texture of their wrappers.

STEAMING

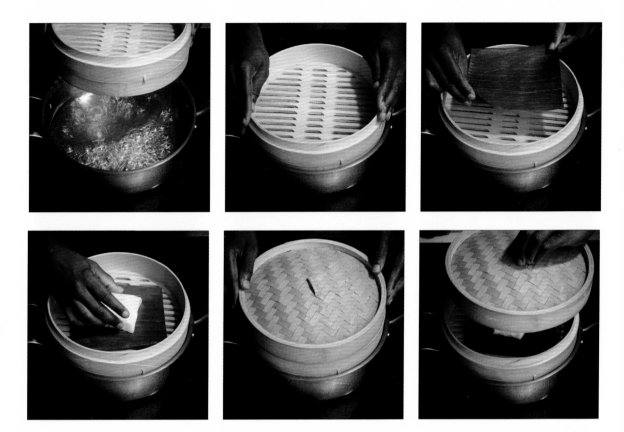

FOR FISH, EITHER WHOLE OR FILLETED

1. To set up a steamer, choose a pan that your bamboo steamer can fit tightly over. Pour 1 to 2 inches of water into the bottom of the pan.

2. Set the top tier of the steamer aside. Cover the pan with the steamer lid and bring the water in the pan to a low boil.

3. Line the bottom tier of the bamboo steamer with a banana leaf or parchment paper. Season the fish with fine sea salt and freshly ground white pepper, then place it on top of the lined steamer tier. (If you have more seafood than fits on the bottom tier of the steamer, line the reserved top tier as well and stack them.) Remove the steamer lid from the pan of boiling water and cover the lined steamer tier.

4. Set the steamer on the pot, making sure that the bottom of the steamer does not touch the water, and keep the water at a low boil to steam. The fish is done cooking when a metal skewer inserted into the middle of the flesh for 5 seconds feels warm when touched to your wrist.

FOR CLAMS, MUSSELS, AND OTHER BIVALVES

1. Place the shells in a large pot with a small amount of liquid, such as wine or broth, and cover.

2. As you heat the pot, the steam from the bivalves' own juices will cook them. When the shells open, they are cooked through. Discard any individual bivalves whose shells do not open after cooking.

HALIBUT EN PAPILLOTE

SERVES 4

4 halibut fillets (7 ounces each), skinned, at room temperature

Fine sea salt and freshly ground white pepper

½ medium onion, cut into ⅛-inch-thick slices

1 large beefsteak tomato, halved through the core and cut into ¼-inch-thick slices

¾ cup dry white wine

4 tablespoons extra-virgin olive oil

8 large fresh basil leaves, chiffonade-cut

SPECIAL EQUIPMENT

Metal skewer

You can cook the fish *en papillote*—enclosed in a parcel made of either aluminum foil or parchment paper—but if you have neither, you can use an ovenproof baking dish with a tightly sealed lid. I like to use foil because the presentation is fun; the trapped steam creates a balloon effect, which looks dramatic when you take the fish out of the oven and serve it. Presenting it this way gives the dish its own charm, though you can remove the fish from the foil or parchment before serving if you wish. If you want to double-check the fish's doneness in the parcel, you can do so by inserting a long, thin metal skewer delicately through the side of the foil or parchment paper and feeling the temperature of the skewer against your wrist.

1. Preheat the oven to 375°F.

2. Cut four 12 × 16-inch pieces of heavy-duty aluminum foil or parchment paper. On a large work surface, fold each piece in half to form a 12 × 8-inch rectangle, then open each like a book.

3. Season the halibut fillets with sea salt and white pepper.

4. Working on the right-hand side of each sheet, set 4 or 5 slices of onion on the foil or parchment, leaving a 1-inch border. Top the onions with tomato slices and lightly season with sea salt and white pepper.

5. Place the seasoned halibut fillets on top of the tomatoes. Crimp the right-hand edges of the foil or parchment around the halibut to form a boat for the liquid, then pour 3 tablespoons of the wine and 1 tablespoon of the olive oil into each packet.

6. Fold the left side of the foil or parchment over the fish and crimp the edges tightly to contain the liquid. Transfer the packets to a large sheet pan.

Recipe continues

7. Cook for 10 to 12 minutes; the parcel should puff up as the steam fills it. Remove the packets from the oven and let rest for 2 to 3 minutes. Open one packet carefully, as steam will escape. Insert a metal skewer into the thickest part of the fish for 5 seconds; it should feel warm when touched to your wrist. If it isn't, reseal the parcel and continue steaming a few minutes longer.

8. When the halibut is finished steaming, transfer each fillet to a warm plate, then spoon the cooked onions and tomatoes over and around the fish. Pour the liquid from the parcel over the fish, garnish with basil, and serve immediately. (Or transfer the packets to plates and serve directly from the foil.)

SNAPPER IN BANANA LEAF
WITH COCONUT-LIME SAUCE
SERVES 4

A technique similar to en papillote, wrapping fish in a banana leaf also adds a distinctive and somewhat exotic flavor to the fish and sauce, slightly herbaceous and earthy. It is best to make as tight a seal as possible to keep the flavors in. You can find banana leaves in many grocery stores, as well as in Asian and Latin American markets and even online. When preparing the vegetables, julienne them very thinly to make sure they cook at the same time as the fish and release their juices into the coconut milk. Add the lime juice as the last step in the sauce—if you add it before cooking, the acidity will kill the other flavors instead of adding a bright contrast.

1 cup full-fat unsweetened coconut milk, such as Chaokoh or Thai Kitchen

1-inch piece fresh ginger, peeled and thinly sliced

1 stalk lemongrass, cut into 1-inch pieces

4 sprigs cilantro

2 limes, 1 juiced and 1 cut into wedges

Fine sea salt and freshly ground white pepper

4 snapper fillets (6 ounces each), skinned

4 (12-inch) squares banana leaf, free from holes or tears

½ large carrot, julienned

½ leek, white parts only, julienned

½ zucchini, julienned

Jasmine Rice (page 69) for serving

1. In a medium pot, combine the coconut milk, ginger, lemongrass, and cilantro. Bring to a simmer and cook for 5 to 7 minutes to infuse the flavors. Add the lime juice and season with sea salt and white pepper. Strain through a fine-mesh sieve into a bowl and set aside.

2. Season the snapper fillets with sea salt and white pepper. Lay a fillet in the center of each banana leaf. Evenly distribute the carrot, leek, and zucchini matchsticks over each piece of snapper, arranging them in nice rows.

3. Spoon a few tablespoons of the coconut milk sauce over the vegetables, then fold the two sides of the banana leaf over the fish, then fold in the top and bottom to form a packet. Secure the flaps with a sturdy toothpick or two.

4. Set up a bamboo steamer: Choose a pan that the steamer will fit tightly over (or use a wok). Pour 1 to 2 inches of water into the pan, cover with the steamer lid, and bring to a simmer over medium-high heat.

SPECIAL EQUIPMENT

Two-tiered 10-inch bamboo steamer

Metal skewer

Recipe continues

5. Place the snapper packets seam side up in the steamer baskets, leaving space between them. Stack the baskets, cover, and carefully place the steamer over the simmering water, making sure the bottom of the steamer does not touch the water.

6. Steam over medium-high heat until a metal skewer inserted into the thickest part of the fish for 5 seconds feels warm when touched to your wrist, 6 to 8 minutes. Turn off the heat and remove the steamer from the pan. Let the snapper packets rest for 3 to 4 minutes.

7. Place a snapper packet on each plate and serve with the jasmine rice and wedges of lime.

JASMINE RICE
MAKES 3 CUPS

1. Place the rice in a bowl and cover with cold water. Let stand for 5 minutes, then drain in a fine-mesh sieve. Rinse until the water runs clear.

1 cup jasmine rice

1 teaspoon fine sea salt

2. In a medium saucepan, bring 1½ cups water to a boil. Stir in the rice and sea salt, return to a simmer, cover, reduce the heat to low, and simmer for 15 minutes. Remove from the heat and let the rice steam, covered, for 5 minutes. Uncover and fluff the rice.

MUSSELS MARINIÈRES ROSÉ

SERVES 4

2 tablespoons extra-virgin olive oil

2 shallots, finely chopped

2 garlic cloves, finely chopped

2 teaspoons all-purpose flour

1 cup rosé wine

3 pounds mussels, scrubbed and debearded

2 tablespoons chopped fresh flat-leaf parsley

Once you buy the mussels, soak them in the sink or a deep bowl of fresh water to remove any sand or dirt, then rinse them before cooking. Check their quality and freshness by smelling them very carefully and discard any bad ones—you'll know by the smell. It takes only one bad mussel to ruin an entire dish. Adding a little flour to the broth gives it texture and richness. Cook this dish à la minute and enjoy it immediately. I always have good bread close by ready to soak up the sauce, and I recommend you do, too!

1. In a large, heavy-bottomed pot (large enough to hold all the mussels), heat the olive oil over medium-high heat. Add the shallots and garlic and sauté until translucent, 2 to 3 minutes. Whisk in the flour a little at a time to form a paste with the olive oil, then add the wine and bring to a boil.

2. Once the wine mixture is boiling, add the mussels, cover the pot, and cook, shaking the pot occasionally, until the mussels open, 5 to 6 minutes. Discard any mussels that don't open, then transfer the rest to a large bowl. Pour the sauce over the top and garnish with parsley. Serve immediately.

CLAMS IN CHORIZO BROTH

SERVES 4

As with all shellfish, thoroughly soak, rinse, and smell the clams, removing any unpleasant ones. This recipe calls for Spanish-style cured chorizo, either spicy or sweet. Cook and serve this straightaway before the clams become cold and chewy. Toasted bread makes an excellent companion for this dish.

24 littleneck or topneck clams

2 tablespoons extra-virgin olive oil

½ cup thinly sliced cured chorizo

1 cup dry white wine

2 tablespoons chopped fresh flat-leaf parsley

1. Rinse the clams, discarding any with broken or open shells.

2. In a large sauté pan, heat the olive oil over medium heat. Add the chorizo and cook until browned, about 3 minutes. Remove from the heat. With a slotted spoon, transfer the chorizo to a large bowl. Set aside.

3. Return the pan to medium-high heat. Add the clams and white wine, cover, and cook, shaking the pan occasionally, until the clams open, 6 to 8 minutes.

4. With a slotted spoon, transfer the clams to the bowl with the chorizo. Strain the hot broth over the clams through a fine-mesh sieve, then garnish with parsley and serve immediately.

HALIBUT-MUSHROOM CASSEROLE

SERVES 4

2 tablespoons unsalted butter

1 tablespoon canola oil

1 pound assorted mushrooms, cut into bite-sized pieces

½ shallot, thinly sliced

Fine sea salt and freshly ground white pepper

2 cups Mushroom Stock (recipe follows)

4 halibut fillets (7 ounces each), skinned

4 sprigs thyme

SPECIAL EQUIPMENT

Metal skewer

This recipe is proof that one-pot dishes can be showstopper meals. Use a medley of different mushrooms to incorporate a variety of textures and nuanced flavors. The earthy mushrooms and savory broth create a surprising contrast that really elevates the delicate flavor of the halibut.

1. Preheat the oven to 375°F.

2. In a large saucepan, heat the butter and oil over medium heat. Add the mushrooms and shallot, season with sea salt and white pepper, and cook until the mushrooms are starting to soften, 4 to 5 minutes. Add the mushroom stock, bring to a simmer, and cook until the liquid is reduced to about 1½ cups, 6 to 8 minutes.

3. Season the halibut on all sides with sea salt and white pepper. Transfer the mushrooms and cooking liquid to a large baking dish and set the halibut on top. Place a thyme sprig on each fillet.

4. Cover the baking dish, place in the oven, and bake until a metal skewer inserted into the thickest part of the fish for 5 seconds feels warm when touched to your wrist, 11 to 12 minutes.

5. To serve, place a fillet in the center of each of four warm bowls. Gently spoon the mushrooms and sauce around the fish and serve immediately.

MUSHROOM STOCK

MAKES 2 CUPS

3 pounds white mushrooms

1. Clean the mushrooms and place in a stockpot with 6 cups water.

2. Bring to a boil, then reduce to low heat and simmer, uncovered, until the liquid is reduced to 2 cups, about 1 hour.

3. Strain through a fine-mesh sieve, pressing the mushrooms to extract the liquid. Refrigerate in an airtight container for up to 1 week or freeze for up to 2 months.

MERLUZA

WITH CURRY OIL AND YELLOW CAULIFLOWER

SERVES 4

Merluza is from the hake family and is thick, flaky, and robust with a delicate flavor. If you are unable to source merluza, hake or even cod will work. Because of the fish's flakiness, take care when lifting it with a spatula so that it doesn't break.

If you don't have a two-tiered steamer, you can cook the cauliflower separately from the fish—just ensure it is tender but still has some bite and texture. I like to add a little lemon juice at the end, as the acidity elevates the fish.

1. Set up a bamboo steamer: Choose a pan that the steamer will fit tightly over (or use a wok). Pour 1 to 2 inches of water into the pan, cover with the steamer lid, and bring to a simmer over medium-high heat.

2. Line the steamer baskets with banana leaves. Put the cauliflower in the bottom basket. Season the merluza fillets with sea salt and white pepper and set them in the top basket. Stack the baskets, cover, and carefully place the steamer over the simmering water, making sure the bottom of the steamer does not touch the water.

3. Steam until a metal skewer inserted into the thickest part of the fish for 5 seconds feels warm when touched to your wrist, 6 to 8 minutes. Turn off the heat and remove the steamer from the pan.

4. Season the cauliflower with sea salt and white pepper. Transfer each fillet to a warm plate, add a serving of the cauliflower alongside, then drizzle with 1 tablespoon of the curry oil. Serve immediately.

Banana leaves, cabbage leaves, or parchment paper for lining the steamer

2 cups yellow cauliflower florets

4 merluza fillets (7 ounces each), skinned

Fine sea salt and freshly ground white pepper

¼ cup Curry Oil (recipe follows)

SPECIAL EQUIPMENT

Two-tiered 10-inch bamboo steamer

Metal skewer

CURRY OIL

MAKES 1 CUP

In a small saucepan, combine the olive oil and curry powder and cook over low heat for 10 to 15 minutes; do not let it boil. Strain the oil through a fine-mesh sieve into a bowl. Store any remaining oil in an airtight container in the refrigerator for up to 3 days.

1 cup light olive oil

1½ tablespoons Madras curry powder

LINGUINE VONGOLE

SERVES 4

40 Manila clams

Fine sea salt

12 ounces linguine

2 tablespoons extra-virgin olive oil, plus more for drizzling

2 garlic cloves, finely chopped

1 cup dry white wine

1 tablespoon finely chopped fresh flat-leaf parsley

½ teaspoon red pepper flakes, plus more, if needed

Juice of ½ lemon, plus more, if needed

I prefer to use Manila clams for this dish, but you can also use cockles, which are slightly smaller. Take care to smell, wash, and rinse the clams and discard any funky ones.

When plating the pasta, try to serve the same number of clams on each plate. Reserve some broth and sprinkle a little over each plate at the end.

1. Rinse the clams, discarding any with broken or open shells. Set aside.

2. Bring a large pot of lightly salted water to a boil over high heat. Add the linguine and cook until tender, 10 to 12 minutes. Drain in a colander.

3. While the pasta cooks, in a large sauté pan, heat the olive oil and garlic over medium heat and cook for 1 to 2 minutes to soften. Add the clams and white wine, cover with a tight-fitting lid, and shake gently. Increase the heat to medium-high and steam until the clams open, 5 to 7 minutes.

4. With a slotted spoon, remove the clams to a large bowl. Add the linguine to the sauce left in the pan and toss to coat. Add the parsley, pepper flakes, and lemon juice and toss again until the pasta is completely coated. Return the clams to the pan, taste, and adjust with sea salt, pepper flakes, or lemon juice if necessary.

5. Divide among four warm bowls, drizzle with olive oil, and serve.

SHRIMP DUMPLINGS

SERVES 4

I particularly like using shrimp for these, but crabmeat also works nicely. It's very important to feel the edge of the dumpling after cooking to check its doneness. The wrapper should be translucent and have a good texture—tender, not firm. I make my own dipping sauce to serve alongside, or sometimes I just use ponzu.

1 pound shrimp, peeled, deveined, and coarsely chopped

Fine sea salt and freshly ground white pepper

¼ cup thinly sliced scallion

¼ cup coarsely chopped fresh cilantro

1 tablespoon grated fresh ginger

1 teaspoon toasted sesame oil

24 round wonton wrappers

Cabbage leaves or parchment paper for lining the steamer

1. Place the chopped shrimp in a bowl and season lightly with sea salt and white pepper. Add the scallions, cilantro, ginger, and sesame oil and stir to combine.

2. Fill a small bowl with warm water and line a sheet pan with wax paper or parchment. Place a wonton wrapper on a work surface and spoon 1 tablespoon of the filling in the center. Wet the edge around the top half of the wonton wrapper using a finger dipped in the water. Pick up the wrapper with both hands. Bring the sides together, forming a half-moon shape that encloses the filling. Pinch the dough together at the center and then make two or three pleats down both sides and press to seal. Transfer the dumpling to the lined sheet pan. Repeat with the remaining wrappers and filling. Cover the dumplings and refrigerate until ready to cook.

3. Set up a bamboo steamer: Choose a pan that the steamer will fit tightly over (or use a wok). Pour 1 to 2 inches of water into the pan, cover with the steamer lid, and bring to a simmer over medium-high heat.

4. Line the steamer baskets with cabbage leaves or parchment with a few holes poked in the paper. Place the dumplings in the steamer baskets, leaving space between them. Stack the baskets, cover, and carefully place the steamer over the simmering water, making sure the bottom of the steamer does not touch the water.

DIPPING SAUCE

¼ cup best-quality soy sauce

¼ cup unseasoned rice vinegar

SPECIAL EQUIPMENT

Two-tiered 10-inch bamboo steamer

Recipe continues

5. Steam until the wrapper is translucent and the shrimp are cooked through, 6 to 8 minutes. Remove from the heat and remove the steamer from the pan.

6. Meanwhile, make the dipping sauce: In a small bowl, combine the soy sauce and rice vinegar and set aside.

7. Transfer the dumplings to a large plate and serve immediately with dipping sauce alongside.

SALMON WRAPPED IN COLLARD GREENS
WITH BEURRE ROUGE
SERVES 4

From the picture, this dish may look sophisticated and complicated, but it is deceptively simple.

If you can't find collard greens, you can use Swiss chard or even spinach, and you can make the sauce in advance. It's essential that each piece of salmon has the same thickness so that they cook evenly, and the timing will differ depending on how you like your fish cooked. The recipe sets a cooking time of 5 minutes for medium-rare salmon, but if you would like to double-check, you can use the skewer test method: Insert a metal skewer through the leaf and into the salmon for 5 seconds, then withdraw the skewer and touch it against your wrist to feel the temperature: *cold = raw, warm = medium-rare to medium, hot = medium-well to well done.*

1. In a small saucepan, combine the red wine, vinegar, shallot, tarragon, and peppercorns. Bring to a boil, then reduce to a simmer and cook until the liquid is reduced to about 6 tablespoons, 6 to 7 minutes. Reserve in the saucepan.

2. Fill a medium stockpot with water and bring to a boil over high heat. Set a large bowl of ice water nearby. Season the boiling water generously with sea salt. Add the collard greens and blanch for 1 minute, then transfer to the bowl of ice water with a slotted spoon. Once cool, remove the collards, gently squeezing them to remove excess water, then transfer to a kitchen towel to drain.

3. Lay the collard greens flat on a large cutting board. Season the salmon pieces with sea salt and white pepper and lay a piece in the center of each collard leaf. Place the mushroom slices over the top of the salmon in a single layer, like shingles. Carefully fold the left side of the collard green over the salmon. Then fold the top of the leaf down, followed by folding the bottom of the leaf up. Roll the salmon toward the final side of the collard, forming a tight package. Repeat

Recipe continues

½ cup dry red wine

½ cup red wine vinegar

1 shallot, minced

4 sprigs tarragon

1 tablespoon black peppercorns

Fine sea salt

4 large collard green leaves, rinsed, large stems trimmed

4 salmon fillets (6 ounces each), skinned and pin bones removed, cut into even 4 × 2 × 1¼-inch rectangles

Freshly ground white pepper

8 white button mushrooms, cut into ¼-inch-thick slices

6 tablespoons cold unsalted butter, cut into pieces

SPECIAL EQUIPMENT

Two-tiered 10-inch bamboo steamer

Metal skewer

with the rest of the collards and salmon pieces, then set them seam side down in the steamer baskets.

4. Set up a bamboo steamer: Choose a pan that the steamer will fit tightly over (or use a wok). Pour 1 to 2 inches of water into the pan, cover with the steamer lid, and bring to a simmer over medium-high heat.

5. Stack the baskets, cover, and carefully place the steamer over the simmering water, making sure the bottom of the steamer does not touch the water. Steam until a metal skewer inserted into the thickest part of the fish for 5 seconds feels warm when touched to your wrist, 4 to 5 minutes. Turn off the heat and remove the steamer from the pan.

6. While the salmon cooks, bring the red wine sauce in the saucepan back to a simmer over medium heat. Whisk in the butter, 1 piece at a time, until fully emulsified. Season to taste with sea salt and white pepper. Strain the sauce through a fine-mesh sieve.

7. Spoon the warm sauce onto each of four rimmed plates to coat the bottom. Slice each salmon package in half and set both in the middle of the plate. Serve immediately.

WARM SKATE SALAD

SERVES 2

Cabbage leaves or parchment paper for lining the steamer

2 boneless, skinless skate wings (7 ounces each)

Fine sea salt and freshly ground white pepper

3 cups mesclun

3 to 4 tablespoons Red Wine Vinaigrette (page 88)

½ tomato, seeded and cut into ⅛-inch dice, for garnish

SPECIAL EQUIPMENT

Two-tiered 10-inch bamboo steamer

The beauty of this dish is the contrast between the warm skate and the cold salad. As the presentation for this dish can be time-consuming—separating the "ribs" of the skate and arranging them rosette-style around the salad—I recommend trying this for two people on your first go and increasing the number of servings as you gain more confidence. Skate can develop a tough texture and lose its flavor once it goes cold, so after plating it around the salad, I like to flash it quickly in a hot oven to warm it up—but only for a few seconds, 10 to 15 max, so as not to wilt the salad. Note that fresh skate flesh should have no redness, and you should not be able to detect any ammonia smell.

1. Set up a bamboo steamer: Choose a pan that the steamer will fit tightly over (or use a wok). Pour 1 to 2 inches of water into the pan, cover with the steamer lid, and bring to a simmer over medium-high heat.

2. Line the steamer baskets with cabbage leaves (or parchment with a few small holes poked in the paper). Season the skate with sea salt and white pepper and place it in one or both baskets. Stack the baskets, cover, and carefully place the steamer over the simmering water, making sure the bottom of the steamer does not touch the water.

3. Steam until the tip of a knife can easily separate the creases in the fish, 4 to 6 minutes. Turn off the heat and remove the steamer from the pan. Let cool slightly.

4. In a bowl, toss the mesclun with 2 to 3 tablespoons of the vinaigrette, then arrange the salad in tall mounds in the center of two dinner plates.

Recipe continues

5. When the skate is cool enough to handle, separate it into thin ribbons, following the natural creases in the fish. Drape the ribbons over the salad in a circle like a tent.

6. Drizzle a little more vinaigrette over the fish, garnish with diced tomato, and serve immediately.

RED WINE VINAIGRETTE
MAKES ABOUT 1 CUP

2 tablespoons red wine vinegar

2 tablespoons sherry vinegar

Fine sea salt

2 teaspoons Dijon mustard

⅓ cup canola oil

⅓ cup extra-virgin olive oil

1 tablespoon finely chopped fresh tarragon

In a medium bowl, combine both vinegars with a pinch of sea salt and stir. Add the mustard, then slowly whisk in the canola oil and extra-virgin olive oil to emulsify. Stir in the tarragon. Cover and set the vinaigrette aside until ready to use. Store any remaining vinaigrette in an airtight container in the refrigerator for up to 3 days.

BLACK BASS
WITH TEA-CITRUS INFUSION
SERVES 4

This is a very light and brightly flavored dish. The harmonious contrast between the tea and the citrus balances perfectly with the pleasant taste of the skin-on steamed black bass. The broth should be clear, so pour it to the side of the fish, not over it, so as to avoid making the broth cloudy.

1. Lay the black bass fillets on a cutting board skin side up. With a sharp knife, make a few slits in the skin to help prevent the fish from curling up when cooked.

2. Season the fillets on both sides with sea salt and white pepper. Line two steamer baskets with cabbage leaves (or parchment with a few holes poked in the paper). Divide the scallions between the baskets, then lay the fish on top.

3. Set up a bamboo steamer: Choose a wide pot that your steamer can fit tightly over. In the pot, combine the ginger, coriander seeds, white peppercorns, and 2¼ cups water and bring to a simmer. Add the black tea leaves.

4. Stack the baskets, cover, and carefully place the steamer over the simmering tea, making sure the bottom of the steamer does not touch the liquid. Steam until a metal skewer inserted into the thickest part of the fish for 5 seconds feels warm when touched to your wrist, 5 to 7 minutes.

5. While the fish cooks, segment the citrus: Cut a thin slice off the top and bottom of the orange. Stand it upright on a cutting board. Following the contour of the fruit, cut downward to remove the peel, pith, and thin white membrane in wide strips, exposing the fruit. Holding the orange in your nondominant hand, use a paring knife to cut along both sides of each section to free it from the membranes, letting the sections fall into a bowl. Repeat with the lemon and lime.

Recipe continues

4 skin-on black bass fillets (7 ounces each)

Fine sea salt and freshly ground white pepper

Cabbage leaves or parchment paper for lining the steamer

12 scallions, white and light green parts only

1-inch piece fresh ginger, peeled and thinly sliced

1½ tablespoons coriander seeds

1 teaspoon white peppercorns

4 teaspoons black tea leaves

1 orange

1 lemon

1 lime

1 tablespoon honey

SPECIAL EQUIPMENT

Two-tiered 10-inch bamboo steamer

Metal skewer

6. Turn off the heat and remove the steamer from the pan. Strain the tea into a small sauce pot and whisk in the honey. Season with sea salt and white pepper.

7. Transfer the fish to wide bowls and pour the tea to the side of the fish. Add the citrus segments to the bowls, garnish with the steamed scallions, and serve immediately.

3 POACHED

POACH

To cook by simmering gently in liquid kept just under the boiling point

There are three ways to poach fish:

- In water or a thin broth
- In a thick neutral liquid or velouté
- In a fragrant sauce, soup, or stew

My favorite way to poach fish is in a thicker liquid, like a velouté, as the denser consistency encases the fish and traps its juices, resulting in a more flavorful fish. Poaching fish in water or broth, though it makes for a lighter dish, can be a little less flavorful. If you do choose to poach in water, take care not to immerse the fish too much, and keep the temperature low to prevent the fish from curling and contracting. Poaching in a small amount of liquid also allows you to observe the fish in the pan more easily, while stopping it from floating around, which can often cause the flesh to break up. Turn the fish throughout the poaching process to make sure it cooks evenly. Nicely poached fish should be moist with a shine, once removed from the liquid.

POACHING

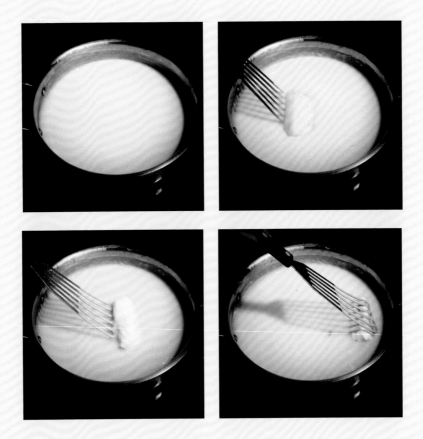

1. Choose a pot big enough that all the pieces of fish will fit inside without touching. Fill the pot with enough poaching liquid to cover the fish completely.

2. Heat the poaching liquid in the pot to 150°F.

3. Pat the fish dry and season with fine sea salt and freshly ground white pepper.

4. Gently place the fish in the poacher and adjust the heat to maintain temperature.

5. After a few minutes, gently turn the fish over.

6. After 5 to 6 minutes total cooking time, remove a fillet and insert a metal skewer in the thickest part. If there is resistance, return it to the pot.

7. When the fish has firmed up and a skewer inserted into the thickest part for 5 seconds feels warm when touched to your wrist, remove the fish from the poaching liquid, then season lightly with fine sea salt and freshly ground white pepper.

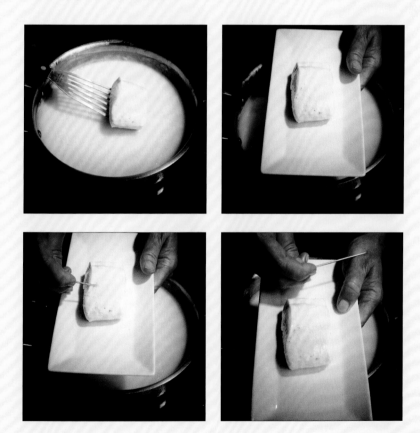

SALMON AND TOMATO À LA GILBERT

SERVES 4

3 medium tomatoes, cored and cut into large chunks, or 1½ cups high-quality canned tomatoes

¼ cup heavy cream

Fine sea salt and freshly ground white pepper

4 salmon fillets (7 ounces each), skinned and pin bones removed, at room temperature

4 sprigs mint

1 teaspoon coarse salt or fleur de sel

SPECIAL EQUIPMENT

Four 1-quart individual covered oval enamelware casseroles or four 1-quart glass cocottes

Metal skewer

When I first I dined at Le Bernardin, Gilbert Le Coze—the chef and co-owner (and my future mentor)—put this dish in front of me. It was the first time I had ever experienced fish that was served to me almost raw, yet was perfectly cooked by the time it was on my fork. Gilbert was famous for creating elegant, elevated, yet simple dishes, and this was a signature of his cooking style: minimal ingredients and steps, maximum impact in terms of flavor and presentation.

While the recipe calls for small individual cocottes or Dutch ovens, you can cook the salmon in one large ovenproof skillet or sauté pan (I recommend one with a glass lid so that you can see the cooking process). The tomato sauce shouldn't cover the salmon but should reach almost to the top edge of the fish without submerging it. The mint (I particularly like using peppermint) adds a powerful aroma, but its flavor also brings a surprising and fresh vibrancy.

1. In a blender or food processor, puree the tomatoes, then strain them through a fine-mesh sieve into a bowl. Stir in the cream and season with sea salt and white pepper. Set aside.

2. Season the salmon fillets lightly with sea salt and white pepper and place one fillet in each of four 1-quart oval enamelware casseroles or glass cocottes. (Or place all 4 fillets in a large sauté pan.) Add the tomato sauce; it should come two-thirds of the way up the sides of the fish.

3. Bring to a full simmer, then divide the mint and coarse salt evenly over the salmon fillets. Cover the casseroles. Remove from the heat and let rest until a metal skewer inserted into the thickest part of the fish for 5 seconds feels warm when touched to your wrist, 6 to 8 minutes.

4. Serve immediately.

MONKFISH BOURRIDE WITH AIOLI

SERVES 4

A fish stew in essence, bourride originated in Sète, a port city in the South of France. The beauty of this rustic dish lies in the balance of local, seasonal ingredients from both land and sea. It is favored by fishermen, who would make it using whatever fish they caught that day, combining it with a flavorful aioli made with garlic that is native to the region and readily available. Take caution when heating the sauce and adding the aioli—keep it at a low simmer as a heavy boil will cause the sauce to break.

1. Make the aioli: In a medium bowl, whisk together the egg yolks and garlic. Add the oil, whisking constantly, drop by drop at first and then in a slow steady stream once the aioli starts to thicken. When all the oil has been incorporated, add the lemon juice and season lightly with sea salt. If the aioli is too thick, add 1 tablespoon water to thin it out. Transfer to a container and refrigerate. (Or substitute with ¾ cup good-quality store-bought mayonnaise combined with 1 clove finely minced garlic.)

2. Prepare the fish: In a large saucepan, simmer the wine until reduced by half, 4 to 5 minutes. Add 4 cups water and return to a simmer. Add the leeks, potatoes, fennel, garlic, and saffron threads and cook until the vegetables are nearly tender, about 8 minutes.

3. Season the monkfish fillets with sea salt and white pepper, then add them to the broth. Cook, covered, for 4 minutes.

4. Add the mussels and shrimp to the saucepan and continue to cook, covered, until the mussels open and the shrimp are opaque, 4 to 5 more minutes. Remove from the heat.

5. Using a slotted spoon, remove the seafood and set aside on a cutting board. Remove the vegetables from the broth with the slotted spoon, dividing them evenly among four warm bowls.

Recipe continues

AIOLI

2 large egg yolks, at room temperature

1 garlic clove, minced

¾ cup light olive oil

2 teaspoons fresh lemon juice

Fine sea salt

FISH

1½ cups dry white wine

2 large leeks, white parts only, halved lengthwise, rinsed, and sliced crosswise ¼ inch thick

2 medium Yukon Gold potatoes, peeled and cut into 12 wedges

1 fennel bulb, trimmed and cut into ¼-inch wedges, fronds reserved for garnish

2 garlic cloves, thinly sliced

1 teaspoon saffron threads

4 monkfish fillets (6 ounces each)

Fine sea salt and freshly ground white pepper

12 large or 16 small mussels, scrubbed and debearded

12 jumbo shrimp (21/25 count), peeled and deveined

6. Bring the broth back to a simmer, whisk in ½ cup aioli and cook for 2 to 3 minutes to thicken. (If there is excess aioli, you can store it in an airtight container in the refrigerator for up to 3 days.)

7. While the sauce is thickening, remove the mussels from their shells and slice the monkfish into ¼-inch-thick rounds.

8. Divide the monkfish, mussels, and shrimp evenly among the bowls. Ladle the sauce over the top, garnish with fennel fronds, and serve immediately.

BLACK BASS WITH NAGE

SERVES 4

Nage is a French term for the classic broth used for poaching. Black bass is a regional fish that can be found from the Carolinas up the Atlantic coast to Massachusetts. It can be difficult to find in the heart of winter, but you can substitute another firm, white fish, such as striped bass or tilefish. The skin is left on in this recipe as it is paper thin, almost an extension of the flesh of the fish, and pleasant to eat. Black bass with its skin on is a perfect fish for poaching or steaming.

1. Make the nage: In a large pot, combine the wine, vinegar, garlic, onion halves, celery, carrot, leek, sea salt, and 10 cups cold water. Bring to a boil, then reduce to a simmer, cover, and cook for 2½ hours.

2. Strain the nage into a large bowl and discard the vegetables. There should be about 10 cups. (If you have less than this, add water to measure 10 cups; if you have substantially more, continue simmering to reduce.) Measure out 1½ cups and set aside for the sauce. Reserve the remainder for poaching the fish.

3. Meanwhile, prepare the vegetables: Bring a medium pot of water to a boil and season generously with sea salt. Set up a large bowl filled with ice water nearby. Add the celery to the pot and after 1 minute add the carrot and leeks. Simmer until the vegetables are soft, 4 to 5 minutes total. Transfer the vegetables to the ice bath. Once cool, drain and set aside.

4. Poach the black bass: Pour at least 2 inches of nage into a large saucepan with straight sides and heat until it reaches 150°F on a thermometer. Season the black bass fillets with sea salt and white pepper, then carefully slide the fish into the liquid. Adjust the heat so that it maintains a temperature of 140° to 150°F as it cooks. Poach the fish until a metal skewer inserted into the thickest part of the fish for 5 seconds feels warm when touched to your wrist, 6 to 8 minutes.

Recipe continues

NAGE

2 cups dry white wine

1 cup champagne vinegar

8 garlic cloves, peeled

2 large onions, peeled and halved

2 celery ribs, quartered

1 medium carrot, peeled and halved

1 medium leek, white and light-green parts only, rinsed and quartered

1 tablespoon fine sea salt

VEGETABLES

Fine sea salt

1 celery rib, cut on the diagonal into ¼-inch pieces

½ medium carrot, cut into ⅛-inch-thick rounds

4 baby leeks, rinsed, tops sliced vertically, keeping the root intact

BLACK BASS

4 skin-on black bass fillets (7 ounces each)

Fine sea salt and freshly ground white pepper

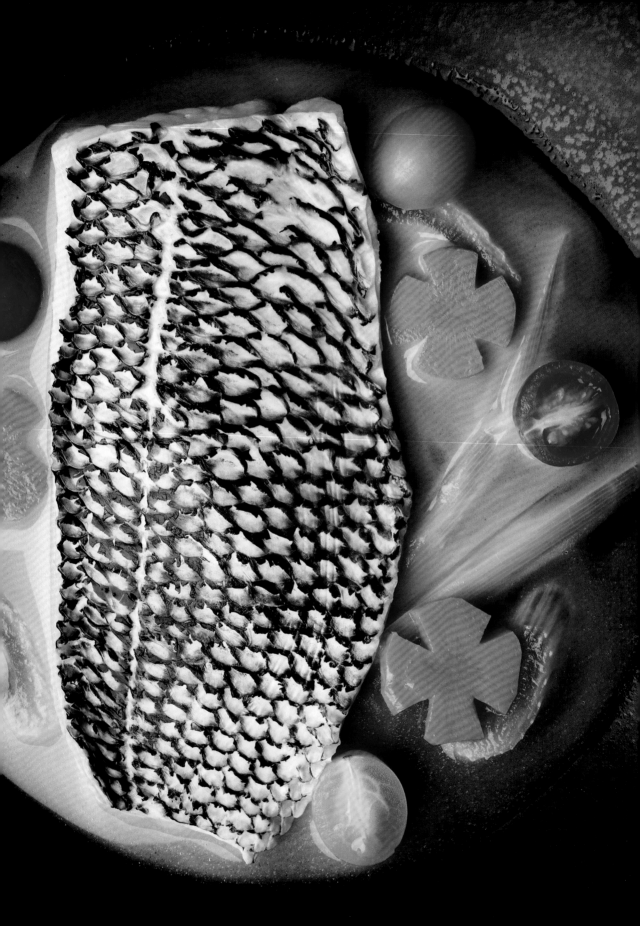

5. To finish: Pour the reserved 1½ cups nage into a small saucepan and bring to a boil. Whisk in the butter, then season with sea salt and white pepper. Keep warm.

6. To serve, place a bass fillet in the center of each of four large bowls, skin side up. Arrange some of the vegetables around the fish, then season the tomato halves with sea salt and white pepper and add them to the bowls. Pour the sauce over and around the fish and serve immediately.

TO FINISH

2 tablespoons unsalted butter

Fine sea salt and freshly ground white pepper

8 multicolored cherry tomatoes, halved

SPECIAL EQUIPMENT

Kitchen thermometer

Metal skewer

SALMON RILLETTES

SERVES 6

2 cups dry white wine

1 tablespoon minced shallot

1 pound fresh salmon fillet, skinned and pin bones removed, cut into 1-inch pieces

3 ounces smoked salmon, skinned and pin bones removed, chopped

½ cup mayonnaise

3 tablespoons fresh lemon juice

2 tablespoons thinly sliced fresh chives

Fine sea salt and freshly ground white pepper

Toasted baguette slices for serving

Salmon rillettes have been welcoming guests to Le Bernardin for many years. More than a canapé, they're a convivial offering that invites guests to share and enjoy—something I hope sets the tone for their dining experience.

It's important that the salmon is cold when you mix it with the mayonnaise; otherwise the sauce will break. You want the mayonnaise to be creamy, not oily. If you are making it from scratch, I recommend grapeseed oil, as it stays emulsified and doesn't congeal when chilled. Add the chives at the last minute so as not to overpower the salmon with a heavy onion taste. You can refrigerate the rillettes (without chives) for up to 2 days, but once the chives are added, the rillettes last only a few hours before they develop an overwhelming onion flavor.

1. Line a plate with a kitchen towel. In a shallow pan, bring the white wine, shallot, and 2 cups water to a boil. Reduce to a simmer and add the fresh salmon. Gently poach the salmon until it is just barely opaque, 2 to 3 minutes.

2. Remove the salmon with a slotted spoon and immediately drain it on the towel-lined plate. Drain the shallot in a small sieve and discard the cooking liquid. Place the salmon and shallot in a bowl and refrigerate until cool.

3. Once the poached salmon and shallot are cool, add the smoked salmon to the bowl, then the mayonnaise and lemon juice, starting with about ¼ cup mayonnaise and adding the lemon juice sparingly. Adjust the levels of mayonnaise and lemon juice to taste as you go. Add the chives and gently mix the rillettes—do not overmix or mix too hard.

4. Season to taste with sea salt and white pepper. Serve cold with toasted baguette slices.

SKATE WITH BROWN BUTTER

SERVES 4

When buying skate wings, make sure there is no redness or blood in the flesh. Skate is an exception to the freshness rule; once it's caught, it should be left for a couple of days before eating. The wing, technically a muscle, can be tough if consumed without aging for a short period. If left too long, though, it will develop an unpleasant ammonia smell. Skate at your local fishmonger will likely have already been aged, but you can refrigerate it for up to 2 days at home; just make sure to monitor it closely.

1. In a medium saucepan, melt 10 tablespoons butter over high heat. Cook, gently shaking the pan, until the butter turns deep brown, 5 to 7 minutes. Remove from the heat and pour the lemon juice into the center of the pan, whisking for about 20 seconds.

2. In a separate saucepan, bring 2 tablespoons water to a simmer. Whisk in the remaining 2 tablespoons butter until fully emulsified. Slowly pour the brown butter into the butter/water emulsion while whisking to fully incorporate. Season with sea salt and white pepper. Set aside and keep warm.

3. Line a large sheet pan with a kitchen towel. In a sauté pan (large enough to hold all the skate wings, or use two pans), combine 3 cups water, the vinegar, and a large pinch of sea salt and bring to a boil. Reduce the heat to low.

4. Season the skate on both sides with sea salt and white pepper and place it in the poaching liquid. The pieces may overlap slightly. Cook until a knife can easily separate the creases in the fish, 3 to 4 minutes.

5. Use a long, wide spatula to remove the skate and drain it on the towel-lined sheet pan.

6. Transfer each piece to a dinner plate. Spoon the brown butter emulsion over and around the skate, completely covering the plate. Sprinkle capers and chives over the skate and serve immediately.

12 tablespoons (1½ sticks) unsalted butter

2 tablespoons fresh lemon juice

Fine sea salt and freshly ground white pepper

½ cup red wine vinegar

4 boneless, skinless skate wings (7 ounces each)

¼ cup drained capers

4 teaspoons thinly sliced fresh chives

POACHED

109

HALIBUT WITH WARM HERB VINAIGRETTE

VELOUTÉ

1 cup all-purpose flour

Juice of 2 lemons

Fine sea salt

VINAIGRETTE

2 tablespoons sherry vinegar

Fine sea salt and freshly
ground white pepper

1 teaspoon Dijon mustard

6 tablespoons extra-virgin
olive oil

¼ cup mixed fresh chives,
parsley, tarragon, and chervil
(fines herbes)

FISH

4 halibut fillets (6 ounces
each), skinned

Fine sea salt and freshly
ground white pepper

12 boiled or steamed jumbo
asparagus spears for serving

SPECIAL EQUIPMENT

Kitchen thermometer

Metal skewer

Halibut is one of the most delicate of fish, in both flavor and texture, and therefore should be handled gently and with great care—overcooking it completely destroys its natural characteristics. To test its doneness, insert a metal skewer through the flesh of the fish until you meet a slight resistance, and leave it for 5 seconds before removing; the skewer should be barely warm when touched to your wrist. (If it's hot, the halibut is overcooked, if cold, not cooked enough.)

Wait until the last moment to chop or mince the herbs and add them to the vinaigrette just before plating to preserve their aromas.

1. Make the velouté: In a wide, shallow pot, bring 7 cups water to a boil over high heat.

2. In a medium bowl, whisk the flour and 1 cup water together until smooth, then whisk the mixture into the boiling water to thicken; it should be the consistency of a milkshake. Add the lemon juice and a generous pinch of sea salt. Reduce the heat to low. The velouté should be hot but not simmering, about 150°F.

3. Make the vinaigrette: Put the sherry vinegar in a bowl and season with a pinch each of sea salt and white pepper, then stir in the mustard. Slowly whisk in the extra-virgin olive oil to emulsify. Chop the herbs and stir them into the vinaigrette. Set aside.

4. Poach the fish: Line a plate or sheet pan with a kitchen towel. Season the halibut fillets with sea salt and white pepper, then place them in the velouté. Cook, turning the fish halfway through, until a metal skewer inserted into the thickest part of the fish for 5 seconds feels warm when touched to your wrist, 8 to 9 minutes.

5. Remove the fillets from the velouté with a slotted spatula to the towel-lined plate or sheet pan. Season lightly with sea salt and white pepper, then transfer the halibut fillets and asparagus to warm plates. Spoon the vinaigrette over and around the fish and serve immediately.

PROVENÇAL FISH STEW

SERVES 4

With its origins in Marseille and the surrounding region, this dish is inspired by a classic bouillabaisse. Fishermen have a great talent for creating delicious, hearty meals with their leftover catch, and this stew is no exception.

Pay special attention to the thicknesses of the various fish and add them to the broth in the according order—the thicker the fish, the more cooking time it needs. For a fresh anise flavor and to tip your hat to a true bouillabaisse, add another splash of Pernod right before serving.

1. In a medium saucepan, heat the olive oil over medium heat. Add the garlic, leeks, fennel, and saffron. Cook until the vegetables start to turn translucent, 3 to 4 minutes. Add the tomato and cook for an additional 2 minutes.

2. Add the Pernod and simmer until reduced by half, about 3 minutes. Add the tomato paste and cook, stirring, for an additional 2 minutes. Add 6 cups water and season with sea salt and white pepper. Bring to a simmer and cook for 15 minutes to infuse the flavors and then reduce the liquid slightly. Strain the broth into a large sauté pan and discard the vegetables. Set on the stove and keep warm.

3. Meanwhile, in a small saucepan, combine the potatoes with water to cover by 1 inch. Season with sea salt and white pepper and bring to a simmer. Cook until the potatoes are easily pierced with the tip of a knife, about 15 minutes. Drain. When the potatoes are cool enough to handle, carefully peel them. Halve the potatoes, then cut each half lengthwise into 4 wedges. Set aside.

4. To serve, bring the broth back to a simmer. Season all the fish with sea salt and white pepper, then gently warm the fillets in the broth for 2 to 3 minutes. Add the shrimp and potatoes and cook until a metal skewer inserted into the thickest part of the fish for 5 seconds feels warm when touched to your wrist, 2 to 3 minutes longer.

5. Divide the fish, shrimp, and potatoes evenly among four soup bowls and pour hot broth over the top. Garnish with fennel fronds, if using, and serve immediately.

3 tablespoons extra-virgin olive oil

6 garlic cloves, thinly sliced

2 medium leeks, white parts only, rinsed and roughly chopped

1 fennel bulb, trimmed and roughly chopped (if your fennel includes fronds, reserve for garnish)

Large pinch of saffron

1 large tomato, roughly chopped

½ cup Pernod

1 tablespoon tomato paste

Fine sea salt and freshly ground white pepper

2 medium Yukon Gold potatoes

8-ounce skin-on black bass fillet, cut into 4 pieces

8-ounce striped bass fillet, skinned, cut into 4 pieces

8-ounce halibut fillet, skinned, cut into 4 pieces

8-ounce snapper fillet, skinned, cut into 4 pieces

4 jumbo shrimp (21/25 count), peeled and deveined

SPECIAL EQUIPMENT
Metal skewer

WARM OCTOPUS CARPACCIO

SERVES 8

Fine sea salt

8 octopus tentacles (from a 4- to 6-pound octopus)

2 teaspoons smoked paprika (spicy pimentón or sweet)

8 tablespoons extra-virgin olive oil

8 teaspoons sherry vinegar

2 tablespoons thinly sliced fresh chives

This preparation really highlights the less-is-more approach to octopus. There is a tendency in many recipes to add too many aromatics (and often some prosciutto) when poaching octopus, and while these additions can bring nice flavors to the broth, they also take away from the uniqueness of the octopus by making it taste meatier rather than enhancing its natural sweetness.

There's a myth that says adding a wine cork to the broth will help tenderize the octopus—I can assure you this is just that, a myth! Please don't add wine corks to your broth!

Octopus should be served warm, as it becomes rubbery and flavorless once it goes cold. Depending on your preference, you can use spicy pimentón or sweet smoked paprika in this recipe.

1. Bring a stockpot half filled with water to a slow simmer and season generously with sea salt. Place the octopus tentacles in the water and cook until the octopus is easily cut with a knife, 2 to 2½ hours. Let cool in the liquid.

2. Preheat the oven to 425°F.

3. When cool enough to handle, slice the tentacles into ¼-inch-thick rounds.

4. Using 1 tentacle per serving, arrange the sliced octopus in a round shape on each of eight ovenproof plates. Season lightly with sea salt and sprinkle with paprika.

5. Warm the plates in the hot oven for 30 to 60 seconds, then remove. Drizzle each serving with 1 tablespoon olive oil and 1 teaspoon sherry vinegar, then sprinkle the chives on top. Serve immediately.

SHRIMP BOIL

SERVES 6 TO 8

I recommend using wild-caught instead of farm-raised shrimp, as they are more flavorful. Do not refrigerate the shrimp after cooking, as they will lose their best qualities. When ready to eat, let the shrimp cool slightly before peeling so that they're warm, not hot, to avoid burning your fingers. I suggest serving with cocktail sauce and hot sauce, and I personally enjoy them with spicy mayonnaise.

1 onion, peeled and quartered

1 head garlic, halved horizontally

3 ribs celery, cut into 3-inch pieces

2 lemons, halved

1 bay leaf

Fine sea salt

½ cup Creole seasoning

1 tablespoon cayenne pepper

3 pounds extra-jumbo shrimp (16/20 count), heads removed

Cocktail sauce, fresh lemon wedges, and hot sauce for serving

1. In a large stockpot, combine 4 quarts water with the onion quarters, garlic, celery, lemon halves, and bay leaf. Add a generous pinch of sea salt and bring to a simmer. Continue simmering for 12 to 15 minutes to let the flavors infuse.

2. Stir in the Creole seasoning and cayenne and return to a simmer.

3. Add the shrimp, cover the pot, and cook at a low simmer until the shrimp are opaque and just cooked through, 5 to 7 minutes. Drain in a colander, discarding the liquid and the aromatics. Transfer the shrimp to a large bowl.

4. Serve with fresh lemon wedges and cocktail and hot sauces.

RED WINE FISHERMAN'S STEW

SERVES 4

¼ cup extra-virgin olive oil, plus more for the toasts

1 small yellow onion, finely chopped

7 garlic cloves, 6 finely chopped and 1 left whole

1 tablespoon tomato paste

4 octopus tentacles (from a 4- to 6-pound octopus)

Fine sea salt and freshly ground white pepper

1 (750 ml) bottle dry red wine

¼ cup finely diced carrot

¼ cup finely diced celery

4 large white mushrooms, quartered

1¾ cups tomato puree

4 small calamari tubes

12 pieces striped bass fillet (2 ounces each), skinned

8 littleneck clams, cleaned and scrubbed

8 long slices country bread

SPECIAL EQUIPMENT

Metal skewer

This is another dish inspired by fishermen, this time from the shores and harbors of Italy. It's similar to my recipe for Provençal Fish Stew (page 113); however, this one is cooked with red wine, which makes it a very friendly dish to drink red wine with. Here I use striped bass, but feel free to add any other seafood you like and that is available to you. As for other dishes of this nature, be aware of the different cooking times for the various types and thicknesses of fish.

1. In a 6-quart saucepan, heat the olive oil over medium-high heat. Add the onion and finely chopped garlic and sauté for 2 to 3 minutes, until the onions are translucent and the garlic is golden. Stir in the tomato paste and cook for an additional minute.

2. Season the octopus with sea salt and white pepper and add to the pot. Add the wine and bring to a simmer. Cover and simmer gently for 1 hour, skimming off any impurities that come to the surface.

3. Preheat the oven to 350°F.

4. Add the carrot, celery, mushrooms, and tomato puree to the pan with the cooked octopus. Return to a simmer, then add the calamari tubes and cook for 10 minutes.

5. Season the striped bass with sea salt and white pepper and add to the pan along with the clams. Cover and simmer without stirring until a metal skewer inserted into the thickest part of the fish for 5 seconds feels warm when touched to your wrist and the clams have opened, 5 to 7 minutes.

6. While the stew finishes, drizzle the slices of country bread with extra-virgin olive oil. Toast in the oven until the bread is golden brown, 3 to 4 minutes. Rub the remaining whole garlic clove over each slice of toast to season it.

7. Carefully ladle the stew into four bowls, dividing the seafood equally. Garnish with toasted bread and serve immediately.

FISH SOUP

SERVES 4 TO 6

This dish is a derivative of fish stew and just as hearty and comforting. You can use any fish except oily fish such as mackerel or bluefish, as they bring too strong a fishy flavor to the soup. I like to top it with croutons with grated Swiss cheese—a favorite addition in our household.

1. Make the aioli: In a small bowl, stir together the saffron and 1 teaspoon warm water and set aside. In a medium bowl, whisk together the egg yolks and garlic. Add the light olive oil, whisking constantly, drop by drop at first and then in a slow, steady stream once the aioli starts to thicken. When all the oil has been incorporated, add the lemon juice and saffron water, and season lightly with sea salt. (Or substitute with ¾ cup good-quality store-bought mayonnaise combined with 1 clove finely minced garlic and a large pinch of saffron.)

2. Make the soup: In a large heavy-bottomed pot, heat the extra-virgin olive oil over medium heat. Add the onion, fennel, and garlic and sauté for 5 minutes. Stir in the saffron and cook until the vegetables are softened and translucent, about 5 minutes.

3. Crush the tomatoes with a fork and add them to the pot along with the Pernod and bay leaf. Season the fish with sea salt and white pepper and add it to the pot. Add enough water to cover the fish by 1 inch, bring to a simmer, and cook for 25 minutes. Remove from the heat and let stand for 5 minutes. Remove the bay leaf.

4. Strain the broth through a colander into a pot. Puree the fish and vegetables in batches in a food mill and whisk the puree back into the broth. Season with sea salt and white pepper. Keep warm.

5. Preheat the oven to 350°F.

6. Spread the baguette slices on a sheet pan and toast in the oven. Coat the toasts with aioli.

7. Bring the soup back to a simmer, then divide it among warm bowls. Garnish with the aioli-slathered baguette and serve immediately.

AIOLI

Large pinch of saffron threads, crumbled

2 large egg yolks, at room temperature

1 garlic clove, minced

¾ cup light olive oil

2 teaspoons fresh lemon juice

Fine sea salt

SOUP

½ cup extra-virgin olive oil

1 medium onion, thinly sliced

½ fennel bulb, trimmed and thinly sliced

4 garlic cloves, chopped

2 teaspoons saffron threads

3 cups canned whole tomatoes with their juice

¼ cup Pernod

1 bay leaf

2 pounds hake fillets, skinned, cut into chunks (or ask your fishmonger for lean white fish scraps)

Fine sea salt and freshly ground white pepper

12 slices (¼ inch thick) baguette

SPECIAL EQUIPMENT

Food mill

4

FRIED

FRY

To cook in hot fat or oil over high heat

There's a special satisfaction from biting into a piece of perfectly fried fish that is hard to match. While techniques such as poaching and steaming will produce dishes that seem similar—both methods create tender, moist flesh—frying is unique, as it produces an end result that can't be achieved any other way. Batter not only gives seafood a crunchy outer texture, it also protects it from the hot oil it's being cooked in, allowing it to stay juicy inside. If fried at the correct temperature and drained well once cooked, fried fish should have little or no residual oil or grease. You will have succeeded in making perfectly fried fish if it emerges ungreasy—it's not just that too much grease is unhealthy, it also kills the flavor.

FRYING

1. To set up a fryer, pour about 3 inches of a neutral oil such as canola oil into a deep straight-sided pot or Dutch oven, filling it less than halfway. Clip a deep-fry / candy thermometer to the side of the pot and preheat the oil to 350°F. Line a plate or sheet pan with paper towels or a kitchen towel.

2. Season the seafood with fine sea salt and freshly ground white pepper. Let stand for 1 minute, then pour in enough milk to cover. Let stand for another minute, then strain.

3. Put the strained seafood in a bowl, add flour, and stir until well coated. Return the seafood to a clean strainer and shake off the excess flour.

4. Working in batches so as not to overcrowd the pot, carefully add the seafood to the hot oil. Adjust the heat to maintain temperature and cook until golden and crisp.

5. Remove the seafood with a slotted spoon or sieve and drain on the towel-lined plate. Season to taste with fine sea salt and freshly ground white pepper, if necessary.

CALAMARI WITH RÉMOULADE SAUCE

SERVES 4

This is an unusual twist on fried calamari as the squid is cut into squares instead of the traditional rings, which not only makes each piece more tender but also makes more sense, eating-wise. It's best to eat the calamari when they're straight out of the fryer. Don't pile them on top of one another as the moisture will make them soggy. Lay them as flat as possible for ultimate crunchiness.

1. Make the rémoulade: In a small bowl, whisk together the mayonnaise and milk. Whisk in the vinegar and lemon juice until well combined. Stir in the chives and cornichon and season to taste with sea salt and white pepper. Transfer to an airtight container and refrigerate for up to 3 days.

2. To set up a fryer, pour about 3 inches of canola oil into a deep straight-sided pot or Dutch oven, filling it less than halfway. Clip a deep-fry / candy thermometer to the side of the pot and preheat the oil to 350°F. Line a bowl with paper towels.

3. Cook the calamari: Put the calamari in a bowl and season lightly with sea salt and white pepper. Let stand for 1 minute, then pour in the milk. Let stand for another minute, then strain. Add the strained calamari to a bowl with the flour and stir until well coated. Return the calamari to a clean strainer and shake off the excess flour.

4. Carefully add half the calamari to the fryer and cook until golden and crisp, 2 to 3 minutes. Remove the calamari with a slotted spoon or a sieve and drain in the towel-lined bowl, then transfer to a plate. Repeat with the remaining calamari.

5. Taste and season with sea salt and white pepper if necessary. Serve immediately with the rémoulade sauce and lemon wedges on the side for squeezing.

RÉMOULADE

½ cup mayonnaise

1 tablespoon whole milk

2 teaspoons red wine vinegar

2 teaspoons fresh lemon juice

2 teaspoons thinly sliced fresh chives

2 teaspoons finely chopped cornichon

Fine sea salt and freshly ground white pepper

CALAMARI

Canola oil for deep-frying

1¼ pounds calamari tubes, rinsed and cut into 1-inch squares

Fine sea salt and freshly ground white pepper

½ cup whole milk

1 cup all-purpose flour

1 lemon, cut into wedges, for serving

SPECIAL EQUIPMENT

Deep-fry / candy thermometer

CRAB CAKE SANDWICHES

SERVES 4

1½ pounds jumbo lump crabmeat, picked over to remove bits of shell or cartilage

Fine sea salt and freshly ground white pepper

1 tablespoon Dijon mustard

2 teaspoons fresh lemon juice

1 cup panko bread crumbs, plus more for coating

⅓ cup plus 4 tablespoons mayonnaise

Canola oil for deep-frying

4 hamburger buns, split

1 beefsteak tomato, cut horizontally into ½-inch-thick slices

8 Bibb lettuce leaves

SPECIAL EQUIPMENT

Four 3½-inch ring molds

Deep-fry / candy thermometer

I like to use jumbo lump crab in this recipe, but you can use any crabmeat; just be sure you remove any bits of shell or cartilage (gently press the crab through your fingers to look for hard pieces, being careful not to break up the meat too much). Panko has more texture than regular bread crumbs and gives the illusion of lightness, but any type of bread crumbs will work. The crab cake should be about an inch thick, warm in the center and golden on the outside.

1. Preheat the oven to 350°F.

2. Put the crab in a bowl and season lightly with sea salt and white pepper. Add the mustard, lemon juice, panko, and ⅓ cup of the mayonnaise. Gently stir to evenly coat the crab, being careful not to break up the crabmeat too much.

3. Divide the crab mixture into 4 portions. Pack each portion tightly in a 3½-inch ring mold.

4. Spread some panko in a shallow dish. Gently remove the crab cakes from the ring molds and coat them well in panko, pressing evenly to coat. Keep refrigerated until ready to use.

5. To set up a fryer, pour about 3 inches of canola oil into a deep straight-sided pot or Dutch oven, filling it less than halfway. Clip a deep-fry / candy thermometer to the side of the pot and preheat the oil to 350°F. Line a plate with paper towels.

6. Gently lower the crab cakes, one at a time, into the hot oil and fry until golden brown, 3 to 4 minutes. Remove with a slotted spoon or a sieve and transfer to the paper towels to drain.

7. Toast the buns in the oven until golden brown, 3 to 4 minutes.

8. To assemble, season the tomato slices lightly with sea salt and white pepper. Spread 1 tablespoon mayonnaise on the bottom of each bun, then top with 2 lettuce leaves. Add a warm crab cake along with a tomato slice to each, cover with the top bun, and serve.

FRIED WHITEBAIT

SERVES 4

Make sure your whitebait (also known as smelts) are fresh. The smaller the fish the better, so you should be looking for around 22 fish per pound. Once cooked, don't overcrowd the plate, as the steam will quickly make the fish mushy.

Canola oil for deep-frying

2 pounds small (16 to 22 per pound) smelts or whitebait

Fine sea salt and freshly ground white pepper

1 cup all-purpose flour

1 tablespoon cornstarch

½ lemon, for juicing, plus 4 lemon wedges for serving

SPECIAL EQUIPMENT

Deep-fry / candy thermometer

1. To set up a fryer, pour about 3 inches of canola oil into a deep straight-sided pot or Dutch oven, filling it less than halfway. Clip a deep-fry / candy thermometer to the side of the pot and preheat the oil to 350°F. Line a sheet pan with paper towels.

2. Rinse the fish under cold running water and drain well. Season lightly with sea salt and white pepper.

3. In a large bowl, combine the flour and cornstarch with a pinch each of sea salt and white pepper. Dredge the fish in the seasoned flour to completely coat and then shake off any excess.

4. Gently add half the fish to the fryer and cook until golden brown, 2 to 3 minutes. Remove with a slotted spoon or a sieve and transfer to the paper towels to drain. Season lightly with sea salt and white pepper. Repeat with the remaining smelts, then squeeze lemon over the top.

5. Serve hot with lemon wedges.

SALT COD FRITTERS

SERVES 4

1 pound salt cod

2 cups all-purpose flour

2 tablespoons baking powder

1 teaspoon fine sea salt

3 large eggs

2 scallions, finely chopped

1 jalapeño pepper, seeded and finely chopped

Canola oil for deep-frying

SPECIAL EQUIPMENT

Deep-fry / candy thermometer

The key to great bacalao, also known as salt cod or salted codfish, is the thickness of the fish; if the flesh is too thin, the salt will overwhelm it. It should be light in color, not gray, and you don't want it to be too pungent. Take the time to thoroughly desalt the fish by rinsing and soaking it. While time-consuming, it's a necessary and very easy step. If you are feeling adventurous, you can make the bacalao by packing fresh cod in kosher salt and leaving it covered to cure for 2 to 3 days. Remove the cod from the salt and then follow the steps in the recipe below.

1. Rinse the fish thoroughly and place it in a bowl of water. Cover the bowl and refrigerate for 3 hours. Drain the water, cover the fish with fresh water, and soak for another 3 hours.

2. After the second soak, drain the water and put the salt cod in a medium pot. Cover with water, bring to a simmer, and cook for 10 minutes.

3. Transfer the fish to a bowl to cool. Break the fish into bite-sized pieces, removing any bones, and set aside.

4. To make the batter, in a large bowl, combine the flour, baking powder, and sea salt. In a separate bowl, beat the eggs, then whisk in ¾ cup water. Gently combine the egg mixture with the flour.

5. Fold the cod, scallions, and jalapeño into the batter; the mixture should be thick and lumpy.

6. To set up a fryer, pour about 3 inches of canola oil into a deep straight-sided pot or Dutch oven, filling it less than halfway. Clip a deep-fry / candy thermometer to the side of the pot and preheat the oil to 350°F. Line a sheet pan with paper towels.

7. Working quickly, use a large spoon to scoop 1-tablespoon portions of the cod mixture and gently place in the hot oil, starting with a total of 8 fritters. The batter will sink at first and then float to the surface. Fry until golden brown, turning the fritters once, 2 to 3 minutes. Remove with a slotted spoon or a sieve and transfer to the paper towels to drain. Repeat with the remaining batter. Serve immediately.

SHRIMP TEMPURA

SERVES 4

DIPPING SAUCE

1 cup dashi, homemade
(page 137) or made with
HonDashi (instant dashi)

¼ cup mirin

¼ cup soy sauce

TEMPURA

Canola oil for deep-frying

1 large egg

¾ cup plus 2 tablespoons
ice-cold water

Fine sea salt

⅓ cup all-purpose flour

⅓ cup rice flour

24 jumbo shrimp
(21/25 count), peeled and
deveined

Grated daikon for serving
(optional)

SPECIAL EQUIPMENT

Deep-fry / candy
thermometer

Mixing rice flour into all-purpose flour helps keep the tempura batter light. When making the batter, make sure to incorporate the dry ingredients into the wet ingredients. It should be a little lumpy and not overmixed, which would activate the gluten and result in a chewy and gooey batter, when we want it to be light and crispy. A spicy mayonnaise dipping sauce would also work nicely with the shrimp, or if you find a mayo-based sauce too rich, ponzu is another great option.

1. Make the dipping sauce: In a small saucepan, combine the dashi, mirin, and soy sauce and bring to a simmer. Remove from the heat and let cool.

2. Prepare the tempura: To set up a fryer, pour about 3 inches of canola oil into a deep straight-sided pot or Dutch oven, filling it less than halfway. Clip a deep-fry / candy thermometer to the side of the pot and preheat the oil to 355°F. Line a sheet pan with paper towels.

3. In a large bowl, combine the egg, the ice water, and a pinch of sea salt.

4. When ready to cook, add the all-purpose and rice flours to the bowl with the wet ingredients and gently mix for 20 seconds. The batter should remain somewhat lumpy.

5. Season the shrimp with sea salt. Dip a shrimp in the batter and gently transfer it to the fryer. Repeat this step with 5 more shrimp. Fry until golden, 1½ to 2 minutes. Remove with a slotted spoon or a sieve and transfer to the paper towels to drain. Repeat in batches with the remaining shrimp.

6. Serve the shrimp with the dipping sauce and a small mound of grated daikon (if using).

DASHI
MAKES ABOUT 1½ CUPS

1. In a small saucepan, bring the kombu and 1½ cups cold water to a simmer and cook for 5 to 7 minutes to let the flavor infuse.

2. Remove from the heat and discard the kombu. Add the bonito flakes and steep for 10 to 12 minutes.

3. Strain the dashi through a fine-mesh sieve into a measuring cup, pressing on the bonito flakes to remove as much liquid as possible. Discard the bonito flakes. Store any remaining dashi in an airtight container in the refrigerator for up to 3 days.

1 (2-inch-square) piece kombu

½ cup shaved bonito flakes

FRIED

SKATE WITH SAMBAL

SERVES 4

SAMBAL

½ cup dried red chiles, preferably Thai, stemmed and seeded

¼ cup small dried shrimp

4 garlic cloves, peeled

1 shallot, roughly chopped

3-inch piece fresh ginger, peeled and thinly sliced

½ stalk lemongrass (plump bottom half), trimmed and thinly sliced

1 tablespoon tamarind paste

½ cup canola oil

⅓ cup sugar

½ cup distilled white vinegar

1 tablespoon cornstarch

Fine sea salt and freshly ground white pepper

SKATE

4 boneless, skinless skate wings (7 ounces each)

Fine sea salt and freshly ground white pepper

1 cup all-purpose flour

Canola oil for shallow-frying

2 to 3 sprigs cilantro, leaves picked and torn, for garnish

2 to 3 sprigs mint, leaves picked and torn, for garnish

Lime wedges for serving

SPECIAL EQUIPMENT

Pastry brush

This is an atypical way to prepare skate. I love the combination of the different textures: the crunchy outside, the creamy flesh, and the sticky, sweet, and spicy contrast of the glaze. Adding lime juice at the end cuts through the richness of the dish.

1. Make the sambal: Soak the chiles and shrimp in separate bowls of water for 10 minutes. Drain.

2. In a high-powered blender or mini food processor, combine the chiles, shrimp, garlic, shallot, ginger, lemongrass, tamarind, and ¼ cup water. Pulse until coarsely pureed but not smooth.

3. In a heavy-bottomed medium pot, heat the canola oil over medium heat. Add the chile puree and cook, stirring frequently, until dark red and thickened, 10 to 12 minutes.

4. Add the sugar and stir until dissolved. Add the vinegar and ½ cup water and bring to a boil. In a small bowl, stir 2 tablespoons water into the cornstarch. Whisk the cornstarch mixture into the sauce and simmer for 2 minutes to thicken. Season with sea salt and white pepper. Transfer to a container to cool.

5. Prepare the skate: Season the wings with sea salt and white pepper. Dredge in flour and set aside. Line a sheet pan with paper towels.

6. Place two large sauté pans over medium-high heat and add ¼ inch of canola oil to each. When the oil is hot but not smoking, gently lay the skate wings in the pans one at a time, 2 wings per pan.

7. Cook until the bottom is golden brown, 2 to 3 minutes. Gently turn over and cook for another 2 to 3 minutes. When crispy on both sides, transfer the skate to the paper towels briefly to remove excess oil.

8. Transfer to warm dinner plates and immediately paint the skate with the sambal using a pastry brush. Garnish with cilantro and mint. Serve with lime wedges and more sambal on the side.

LOBSTER SPRING ROLLS

SERVES 4

I love the adaptability of this recipe; you can switch out the lobster for crabmeat or cooked shrimp if you prefer, and egg roll wrappers work just as well as rice paper wrappers. Serve warm, not hot, as you'll be eating them with your hands, but enjoy them quickly before they get soggy!

1. Make the dipping sauce: In a small bowl, combine the fish sauce, sugar, ginger, and 6 tablespoons water. Stir to dissolve the sugar, taste, and season with white pepper. Set aside.

2. Make the lobster rolls: In a bowl, combine the lobster meat, carrot, ginger, scallion, and lime zest. Season lightly with sea salt and white pepper. Mix and set aside.

3. Set up a cutting board with a wide, shallow bowl of lukewarm water next to it. Working one at a time, dip a spring roll wrapper in the water until softened, 10 to 20 seconds. Place the softened wrapper on the cutting board. Spoon about ½ cup of the lobster mixture onto the lower third of the wrapper and shape the filling into a horizontal log about 2 inches from the bottom of the wrapper. Fold the bottom edge of the wrapper up over the filling and then fold in the sides to enclose the filling. Roll it into a tight cylinder. Transfer the roll to a sheet pan and repeat with the remaining filling and wrappers.

4. Line a plate with paper towels. Add ¼ inch of canola oil to a large nonstick sauté pan. Put the pan over medium-high heat, and when the oil is hot, add 4 rolls to the pan, one at a time, and shallow-fry the spring rolls until golden brown on all four sides, about 8 minutes, turning the rolls every 2 minutes. Remove the rolls from the pan and set on the paper towels to drain. Repeat with the remaining 4 rolls.

5. To serve, place a warm roll in a lettuce leaf and top with 1 sprig cilantro and some mint leaves. Serve immediately with the dipping sauce.

DIPPING SAUCE

½ cup fish sauce

1 tablespoon sugar

1 tablespoon grated fresh ginger

Freshly ground white pepper

LOBSTER ROLLS

1 pound cooked lobster meat, cut into ¼-inch dice

½ large carrot, peeled and cut into thin matchsticks

1 tablespoon grated fresh ginger

1 tablespoon finely diced scallion

1 teaspoon grated lime zest

Fine sea salt and freshly ground white pepper

8 (9- to 10-inch) spring roll wrappers

Canola oil for shallow-frying

8 Bibb or Boston lettuce leaves

8 sprigs cilantro

8 sprigs mint, leaves picked

FISH FINGERS

SERVES 4

1 cup all-purpose flour

1½ cups panko or regular fine dried bread crumbs

2 large eggs

1½ pounds hake or cod fillets, skinned, cut into about twelve 1 × 3-inch fingers

Fine sea salt and freshly ground white pepper

1 cup broccoli florets

Canola oil for deep-frying

Ketchup

SPECIAL EQUIPMENT

Deep-fry / candy thermometer

A firm favorite of my son, this is a dish big kids will enjoy, too! I like to use panko, but if I'm cooking for younger kids, regular bread crumbs give a softer texture. Ketchup is always popular, but tartar sauce goes excellently with these as well. If your kids enjoy the broccoli served alongside, that's a bonus!

1. Bring a large pot of water to a boil over high heat.

2. Meanwhile, set up a breading station: Place the flour and bread crumbs in separate shallow-rimmed plates. Beat the eggs in a wide, shallow bowl until well combined.

3. Season the fish fingers with sea salt and white pepper, then dredge them in the flour. Shake off any excess, then place them in the egg mixture and coat well. Remove from the egg mixture and gently dredge in the bread crumbs. Place the breaded fish on a sheet pan and keep cool until ready to cook.

4. When the water is boiling, add sea salt and the broccoli florets. Cook for 4 minutes, or until just tender. Drain and keep warm.

5. To set up a fryer, pour about 3 inches of canola oil into a deep straight-sided pot or Dutch oven, filling it less than halfway. Clip a deep-fry / candy thermometer to the side of the pot and preheat the oil to 350°F. Line a sheet pan with paper towels.

6. Gently add half the fish fingers, one at a time, to the hot oil and cook until golden brown, 3 to 4 minutes. Remove with a slotted spoon or a sieve and transfer to the paper towels to drain. Repeat with the remaining fish fingers.

7. Divide the fish fingers and broccoli among four plates. Serve with ketchup on the side.

FISH TACOS

SERVES 4

There are many ways to make fish tacos: fried, grilled, or sometimes even steamed. There is just something unmatched about the combination of the crunchy texture of batter-fried fish, creamy guacamole, sharp salsa, and soft, warm tortillas. I recommend cod or hake here, but any non-oily white fish, such as halibut, works well, too.

1. Make the guacamole: Scoop the avocado flesh into a bowl. Crush the avocado, then stir in the cilantro and lime juice. Season to taste with sea salt and white pepper. Cover and keep cool.

2. Make the salsa: In a bowl, combine the tomatoes, onion, jalapeño, cilantro, lime juice, and sea salt and white pepper to taste. Cover and set aside.

3. To set up a fryer, pour about 3 inches of canola oil into a deep straight-sided pot or Dutch oven, filling it less than halfway. Clip a deep-fry / candy thermometer to the side of the pot and preheat the oil to 350°F. Line a sheet pan with paper towels.

4. Fry the fish: Season the cod with sea salt and white pepper and set aside. Combine the flour and cornstarch in a bowl. Slowly whisk in the sparkling water, then season lightly with sea salt and white pepper.

5. Working in batches, dip the cod pieces in the batter to completely coat. Gently add them to the fryer, one piece at a time, and cook until golden brown and crunchy, 3 to 4 minutes. Remove with a slotted spoon and transfer to the paper towels to drain. Remove extra batter from the fryer with a slotted spoon between batches. Repeat with the remaining fish.

6. Place a large sauté pan or cast-iron skillet over medium-high heat. Add a tortilla to the pan and quickly char, turning after 20 to 30 seconds. Repeat with the remaining tortillas.

7. To assemble, put 1 tablespoon of guacamole in the center of each tortilla and top with fried cod. Finish with tomato salsa and serve hot.

GUACAMOLE

2 avocados, halved and pitted

2 tablespoons chopped fresh cilantro

2 tablespoons fresh lime juice

Fine sea salt and freshly ground white pepper

SALSA

1 pound Roma tomatoes, seeded and finely chopped

½ small red onion, finely chopped

½ jalapeño pepper, seeded and finely chopped

1½ teaspoons finely chopped fresh cilantro

1½ teaspoons fresh lime juice

Fine sea salt and freshly ground white pepper

FISH

Canola oil for deep-frying

1½ pounds boneless, skinless cod or hake, cut into 8 equal rectangles

Fine sea salt and freshly ground white pepper

1 cup all-purpose flour

1 tablespoon cornstarch

1 cup sparkling water

8 (6-inch) corn tortillas

SPECIAL EQUIPMENT

Deep-fry / candy thermometer

5 BAKED

BAKE

To cook by dry heat in an oven

Baking is an easy technique that doesn't require much equipment. If you don't have access to a regular oven, a small countertop appliance like a toaster oven can suffice. The benefit of cooking fish in an oven is that it allows you to prepare large quantities without too much hassle or too many moving parts. It's a simple way of cooking and probably the friendliest technique for beginners, so long as you pay attention to the temperature and timing and test for doneness.

BAKING

1. Preheat the oven to 400°F.

2. Choose pieces of fish of similar size and thickness to ensure even cooking. Pat the fish dry and season both sides with fine sea salt and freshly ground white pepper.

3. Lightly brush a baking dish with a neutral oil, like canola or vegetable oil, then place the fish on top and gently brush its surface with a small amount of the oil as well.

4. Place in the oven and bake until a metal skewer can be easily inserted into the fish and, when left in for 5 seconds, feels warm when touched to your wrist.

5. Remove from the oven, let rest for a few minutes, and then serve.

SALT-CRUSTED RED SNAPPER

SERVES 4

The beauty of baking the snapper in salt is that the fish is cooked evenly each time and, as an added benefit, seasoned very nicely as well. This is a basic salt-crust recipe, but you can add chopped fresh herbs, such as rosemary or thyme, to add flavor and aroma. When separating the cooked fish from the bone, remove the top fillet first, then gently lift the bones up starting from the tail end; the bones should come away easily to reveal the perfectly cooked bottom fillet.

4½ cups kosher salt

3 large egg whites

1 whole snapper (4 to 5 pounds), scaled, gutted, and gills removed

½ cup extra-virgin olive oil

1 lemon, cut into wedges, for serving

SPECIAL EQUIPMENT

Metal skewer

Pastry brush

1. Preheat the oven to 400°F.

2. In a large bowl, mix the kosher salt, egg whites, and ¼ cup water until well combined. On a sheet pan, spread out one-third of the salt mixture, shaping it into a rectangle that is slightly larger than the fish. Place the fish on top. Cover the fish with the remaining salt mixture and press into shape. The fish should be sealed within the salt crust.

3. Place the pan in the oven and bake for 30 minutes.

4. Remove from the oven and let the fish rest for 10 minutes. A metal skewer inserted through the salt crust into the thickest part of the fish for 5 seconds should feel warm when touched to your wrist.

5. Crack the crust with a spoon and gently remove the salt, using a pastry brush to sweep away any excess. Working from the head to the tail of the fish, use the tip of a knife to gently lift the skin from the flesh and discard. Following the body line in the center of the fish, use a large spatula to lift the fillets from the bones and transfer to a serving platter. Be sure to check for any remaining bones and remove them. Gently grab the tail end of the bone and pull it up toward the head to remove the fish's backbone and ribs. Gently remove the rest of the fish to the platter, leaving the skin behind.

6. Spoon the olive oil over the fillets and serve immediately with lemon wedges.

SALMON WITH HERB-INFUSED EXTRA-VIRGIN OLIVE OIL

SERVES 4

2-pound piece skin-on center-cut salmon fillet, at room temperature

Fine sea salt and freshly ground white pepper

½ cup roughly chopped fresh dill

1 teaspoon grated lemon zest

3 tablespoons extra-virgin olive oil

SPECIAL EQUIPMENT

Metal skewer

This is a recipe that requires a lower oven temperature, as cooking salmon slowly at a low temperature doesn't cause it to release albumin (the white protein you might see when cooked at higher temperatures), and so it remains inside the flesh, making the fish tender and giving it an even consistency when cooked. If your salmon fillet has pin bones, I would recommend removing them after it's cooked, as they are easier to get out. Serve with boiled potatoes or cucumber salad alongside.

1. Season the salmon with sea salt and white pepper and place in a large ovenproof sauté pan or baking dish.

2. In a bowl, combine the dill, lemon zest, and 1 tablespoon of the olive oil and mix well. Spread the dill mixture evenly over the salmon, cover the pan with plastic wrap, and refrigerate for 1 hour.

3. Position a rack in the center of the oven and preheat the oven to 275°F.

4. When ready to cook, remove the plastic wrap and add the remaining 2 tablespoons olive oil to the pan. Place the salmon in the oven and bake until a metal skewer inserted into the thickest part of the fish for 5 seconds feels warm when touched to your wrist, 15 to 18 minutes. Remove from the oven, cover with foil, and let stand for 5 minutes.

5. Remove any pin bones, gently portion the salmon using a sharp knife, and divide it among four warm plates.

WARM SCALLOPS
WITH MUSTARD SAUCE
SERVES 4

Fresh scallops, both raw and cooked, are firm—never soft or chewy. By nature, scallops are sweet, so the tomato confit and mustard sauce bring acidity and contrast that complement their natural flavors beautifully. Overcooking scallops ruins their qualities, so to fully showcase their sweetness and texture, it's important that they be still slightly translucent after cooking.

1. Make the tomato confit: Preheat the oven to 250°F. Line a sheet pan with parchment paper.

2. Halve the tomatoes horizontally. Put the halved tomatoes on the sheet pan, cut side up. Coat the tomato halves with the olive oil, season with sea salt and white pepper, then top them with the thyme sprigs.

3. Bake the tomatoes until they collapse and take on a hint of color, 1 to 1½ hours. Remove the tomatoes from the oven and cool to room temperature. Leave the oven on and increase the temperature to 400°F.

4. When the tomatoes are cool, peel and roughly chop them. Set aside in a saucepan.

5. Make the mustard sauce: In a small saucepan, bring 2 tablespoons water to a simmer over medium heat. Whisk in the butter, 1 tablespoon at a time, to emulsify. Stir in both mustards. Taste and season with sea salt and white pepper. Set aside and keep warm.

6. Cook the scallops: Line a sheet pan with parchment paper and lightly oil the parchment. Slice the scallops horizontally into ¼-inch-thick disks and lay them on the pan in a single layer. Depending on the size of the scallops, there will be 5 to 8 slices per person.

Recipe continues

TOMATO CONFIT

3 large beefsteak tomatoes

¼ cup extra-virgin olive oil

Fine sea salt and freshly ground white pepper

6 sprigs thyme

MUSTARD SAUCE

1 stick (4 ounces) cold unsalted butter, cut into tablespoons

2 teaspoons whole-grain mustard

1 teaspoon Dijon mustard

Fine sea salt and freshly ground white pepper

SCALLOPS

Neutral oil for the pan

10 large sea scallops (about 1 pound total)

Fine sea salt and freshly ground white pepper

SPECIAL EQUIPMENT

Four 5-inch ring molds

7. Heat the tomato confit in its pan, cooking until almost dry, 5 to 7 minutes. Taste for seasoning and adjust if necessary.

8. To serve, place a 5-inch ring mold in the center of each of four warm plates. Evenly divide the tomato confit among the molds, gently pressing down to flatten it.

9. Season the scallops with sea salt and white pepper. Transfer to the oven and quickly heat for 60 to 90 seconds.

10. Remove the ring molds from the plates and carefully overlap the scallop slices on top of the tomato confit. Finish with warm mustard sauce and serve immediately.

SOFRITO-GLAZED MAHIMAHI

SERVES 4

Mahimahi is a fish that hardens and becomes dry quite quickly, so it needs to be cooked swiftly to medium-rare in order to enjoy its natural qualities. It's prepared here with sofrito, an aromatic garnish that can form a sauce or a base to bring flavor to a variety of dishes. There are many ways to make sofrito—the Spanish way is very different from how Puerto Ricans make it, for example—but almost all versions contain garlic, onion, and peppers. In this instance we use sofrito both to flavor the fish itself by painting it on the mahimahi and to make the sauce.

1. Preheat the oven to 400°F.

2. Halve the acorn squash horizontally and remove the seeds. Place the halves cut side up in a baking dish that holds the squash tightly and season with sea salt and white pepper. Add ½ inch water to the baking dish and cover with foil. Bake the acorn squash until tender and easily pierced with a paring knife, 40 to 45 minutes. Remove the squash from the oven and let cool. Leave the oven on.

3. When cool enough to handle, slice the acorn squash into 12 slices about ½ inch thick and 3 inches long. Gently pull off the skin. Set aside in a baking dish or on a sheet pan.

4. In a sauté pan, heat the canola oil over medium heat. Add the bell pepper, onion, garlic, and jalapeño (if using) and cook until soft, 8 to 10 minutes. Transfer the vegetables to a blender with the softened butter and puree at low speed, gradually increasing the speed to form a smooth puree. Remove the sofrito butter from the blender and season with sea salt and white pepper.

5. Season the mahimahi fillets on both sides with sea salt and white pepper and place them in a large baking dish. Using a pastry brush,

1 acorn squash

Fine sea salt and freshly ground white pepper

2 tablespoons canola oil

1 cup sliced red bell pepper or ají dulce

½ small onion, thinly sliced

1 garlic clove, sliced

½ jalapeño pepper (optional), seeded and sliced

1 stick (4 ounces) unsalted butter, at room temperature

4 mahimahi fillets (7 ounces each), skinned, at room temperature

1 tablespoon fresh lime juice

SPECIAL EQUIPMENT

Pastry brush

Metal skewer

Recipe continues

coat the top of each fillet with 1 tablespoon sofrito butter. Pour in enough water (pouring around, not over, the fish) to cover the bottom of the dish by ¼ inch.

6. Slide the baking dish into the oven and bake until a metal skewer inserted into the thickest part of the fish for 5 seconds feels warm when touched to your wrist, 7 to 8 minutes.

7. Meanwhile, in a saucepan, bring 3 tablespoons water to a simmer and whisk in the remaining sofrito butter, a little at a time, until well incorporated. Season the sauce with sea salt and white pepper to taste.

8. After removing the fish from the oven, place the acorn squash slices in the oven for 2 to 3 minutes to warm, then divide them among four warm plates. Transfer the mahimahi fillets to the plates. Stir the lime juice into the sauce at the last minute and pour the sauce around each plate. Serve immediately.

RED SNAPPER
WITH COCONUT-TOMATO SAUCE

SERVES 4

1 tablespoon canola oil

1 tablespoon minced shallot

1½ teaspoons minced fresh ginger

2 garlic cloves, minced

3 tomatoes, seeded and cut into ¼-inch dice

1 cup full-fat unsweetened coconut milk

Fine sea salt and freshly ground white pepper

4 red snapper fillets (7 ounces each), skinned

2 limes, halved and seeded

Caribbean Fried Rice (page 163) for serving

SPECIAL EQUIPMENT

Metal skewer

This is a great recipe to use up your overripe tomatoes, as they will release maximum juice and flavor. Before plating, remove the snapper from the baking dish, spoon the sauce and garnish evenly on the plates, and then top with the fish. The snapper in this preparation can be easily replaced with another white, non-oily fish such as halibut or hake.

1. Preheat the oven to 400°F.

2. In a medium saucepan, heat the canola oil over medium heat. Add the shallot, ginger, and garlic and cook until soft, making sure not to brown them, 8 to 10 minutes.

3. Add the tomatoes and coconut milk and simmer until the tomatoes release their juices, about 5 minutes. Remove from the heat and season with sea salt and white pepper.

4. Transfer the coconut-tomato sauce to a baking dish large enough to hold the snapper fillets in a single layer. Season the fillets with sea salt and white pepper on both sides. Place the snapper in the baking dish.

5. Bake until a metal skewer inserted into the thickest part of the fish for 5 seconds feels warm when touched to your wrist, about 12 minutes.

6. To serve, remove the snapper from the baking dish to a plate, then divide the coconut-tomato sauce among four warm plates and top each with a snapper fillet. Squeeze lime juice over the top. Serve with the fried rice.

CARIBBEAN FRIED RICE

SERVES 4

1. Rinse and drain the basmati rice. Place the rice in a small saucepan with 2⅔ cups water and a pinch of sea salt. Bring the rice to a boil over high heat, reduce the heat to medium, and simmer until most of the water has been absorbed, about 10 minutes. Place a tight-fitting lid on the pan, remove from the heat, and let sit for another 10 minutes. Spread the rice out on a sheet pan and refrigerate. This should yield about 4½ cups cooked rice.

2. In a large nonstick skillet, heat the canola oil over high heat. Add the shrimp to the pan, followed by the ginger and scallions, and very quickly toss until fragrant. Add the rice, pineapple, mango, and apple and season to taste with sea salt, white pepper, and cayenne. Garnish with roughly chopped cilantro and serve hot.

1½ cups basmati rice

Fine sea salt

2 tablespoons canola oil

½ cup ¼-inch-diced shrimp

1 teaspoon minced fresh ginger

3 tablespoons thinly sliced scallions

¼ cup ¼-inch-diced pineapple

¼ cup ¼-inch-diced mango

¼ cup ¼-inch-diced apple

Freshy ground white pepper

Cayenne pepper

Cilantro for garnish

BAKED

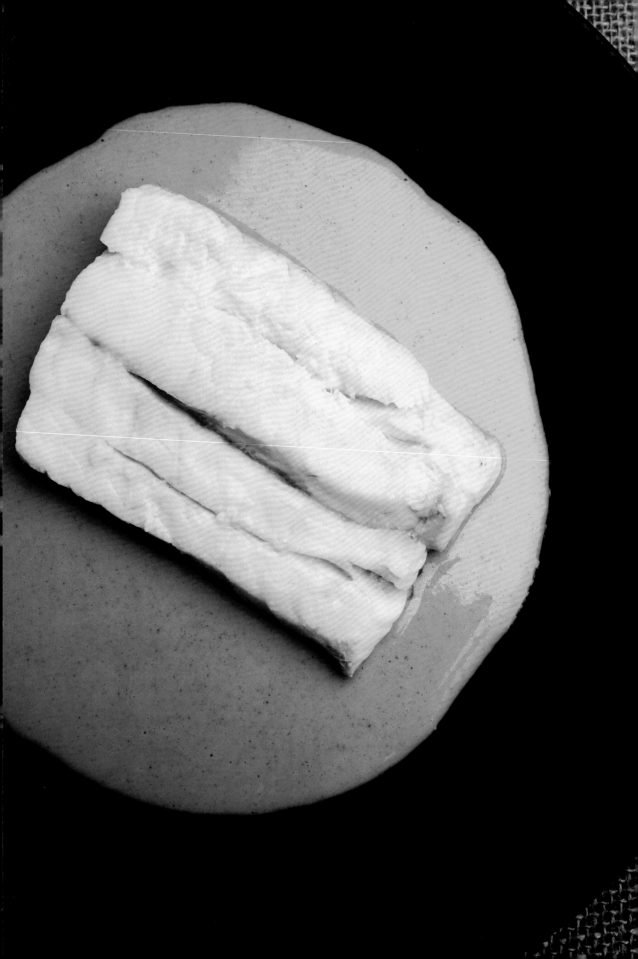

SNAPPER WITH CURRY SAUCE

SERVES 4

Madras is my curry powder of choice here; however, you can use a spicier or more complex curry if you wish. When using curry powder, it's important to cook it well to extract all the essences. Feel free to use water instead of chicken stock, though stock will bring more richness and depth to the sauce.

1. Preheat the oven to 400°F.

2. Make the curry sauce: In a saucepan, heat the canola oil over medium heat. Add the garlic, shallot, lemongrass, and ginger. Cook until starting to soften but not brown, about 5 minutes. Add the curry powder and stir to combine. Add the coconut milk and ½ cup water and simmer for about 10 minutes to let the flavors infuse.

3. Remove the sauce from the heat and strain it through a fine-mesh sieve into a saucepan. Season to taste with sea salt and white pepper. Set aside and keep warm.

4. Prepare the snapper: Season the fillets on both sides with sea salt and white pepper. Butter the bottom of a large baking dish and place the fillets in the dish in a single layer, keeping them evenly spaced. Add enough water to just cover the bottom of the dish, then place it in the oven. Bake the snapper until a metal skewer inserted into the thickest part of the fish for 5 seconds feels warm when touched to your wrist, 7 to 8 minutes.

5. Return the curry sauce to a simmer, then remove from the heat. Spoon the sauce into the center of four warm plates and top with the fish. Squeeze a little lime juice over the fish and sauce and serve immediately.

CURRY SAUCE

2 tablespoons canola oil

2 garlic cloves, thinly sliced

1 shallot, thinly sliced

1 stalk lemongrass, trimmed and roughly chopped

1½ teaspoons minced fresh ginger

2 tablespoons Madras curry powder

1 cup full-fat unsweetened coconut milk

Fine sea salt and freshly ground white pepper

SNAPPER

4 snapper fillets (6 to 7 ounces each), skinned

Fine sea salt and freshly ground white pepper

2 tablespoons softened unsalted butter, for the baking dish

1 lime, halved and seeded

SPECIAL EQUIPMENT

Metal skewer

STRIPED BASS
WITH SWEET ONIONS AND THYME
SERVES 4

ONION CONFIT

1 tablespoon canola oil

3 cups thinly sliced yellow onion

3 tablespoons unsalted butter

Fine sea salt and freshly
ground white pepper

½ cup dry white wine

1 teaspoon fresh thyme leaves

STRIPED BASS

4 striped bass fillets (7 ounces
each), skinned

Fine sea salt and freshly
ground white pepper

4 sprigs thyme

SPECIAL EQUIPMENT

4 small (9-inch) casserole
dishes

Metal skewer

Caramelized onions can be very sweet, and though they are quite light, they often give the illusion of being rich, so if you wish, you can add a splash of lemon juice or red wine vinegar to cut through that perceived richness. There should be enough broth left over for the sauce, but if not, add a little water to increase the liquid.

1. Preheat the oven to 400°F.

2. Make the onion confit: In a large sauté pan, heat the canola oil over medium-high heat. Add the onion and cook, stirring, until the onion softens, 2 to 3 minutes. Reduce the heat to medium and add the butter. Cook until the onion is golden and translucent, about 15 minutes. Season with sea salt and white pepper. Add the wine, ¼ cup water, and the thyme leaves. Bring to a simmer, then remove from the heat.

3. Cook the striped bass: Divide the onion confit among four 9-inch casserole dishes (or use 1 large baking dish). Season both sides of the striped bass with sea salt and white pepper, then place on top of the onions and lay 1 thyme sprig over each piece of fish. Transfer to the oven and bake until a metal skewer inserted into the thickest part of the fish for 5 seconds feels warm when touched to your wrist, 7 to 8 minutes.

4. Remove from the oven and let rest for a few minutes before serving.

FLUKE "PAILLARD"

SERVES 4

The fluke, cooked paillard-style, will come out of the oven very hot, so make sure to add the endive and basil at the very last minute to keep them from wilting and also to retain their bright flavors, colors, and textures.

1. Preheat the oven to 450°F.

2. Spread half the capers on paper towels to dry.

3. In a small skillet, heat the canola oil over medium-high heat. Add the dried capers and quickly fry for 15 to 20 seconds. The capers should puff slightly. Carefully place the capers on more paper towels to drain. Set aside.

4. Season the fluke fillets with sea salt and white pepper on both sides. Rub a little oil on the inside of a large baking dish and place the fillets in a single layer in the dish.

5. In a bowl, toss together the tomatoes, both olives, and remaining uncooked capers and season with sea salt and white pepper. Drizzle with the olive oil and toss again.

6. Cover the fluke fillets with the tomato mixture. Bake until a metal skewer inserted into the thickest part of the fish for 5 seconds feels warm when touched to your wrist, 6 to 7 minutes.

7. Transfer the fluke to warm plates and spoon the tomato mixture over and around the fish. Garnish with sliced endive, basil, and fried capers. Serve immediately.

1½ teaspoons drained capers

1 tablespoon canola oil , plus more for the baking dish

4 fluke fillets (7 ounces each), skinned

Fine sea salt and freshly ground white pepper

12 cherry tomatoes, halved

¼ cup sliced pitted green olives

¼ cup sliced pitted kalamata olives

½ cup extra-virgin olive oil

12 small endive leaves, trimmed and halved lengthwise

4 large fresh basil leaves, chiffonade-cut

SPECIAL EQUIPMENT
Metal skewer

6

SAUTÉED

SAUTÉ

To cook quickly in a small amount of fat or oil in a hot pan over direct heat

You can tell a sautéed fish by the light crust and nice golden color that enhance its flavor. Sautéing is a quick and great way of creating a crust directly on one side of the fish itself, adding texture while keeping the other side moist and soft (creating a crust on both sides can make the fish too dry). Sautéing is also a quick process, so it is particularly effective for shellfish or mollusks (such as calamari), which are sensitive to overcooking. This technique can be key to keeping these kinds of seafood tender and flavorful.

SAUTÉING (PAN-FRYING)

1. Use fish with the skin on. Season both sides with fine sea salt and freshly ground white pepper. Let the fish rest for 20 minutes.

2. Place a medium skillet over high heat until very hot but not smoking and add enough canola oil to coat the bottom of the pan. Pat the skin side of the fish dry, then dust the skin side with Wondra flour.

3. Add the fish to the pan skin side down and briefly press down on it with a metal spatula to prevent the fish's skin from shrinking. Reduce the heat to medium-high and continue to gently press the fish flat. Once flattened, cook the fish until the skin is golden brown and crisp, 3 to 5 minutes.

4. Flip the fish over and cook until a metal skewer can be easily inserted into the fish and, when left in for 5 seconds, feels just warm when touched to your wrist, about 1 minute. Remove from the pan.

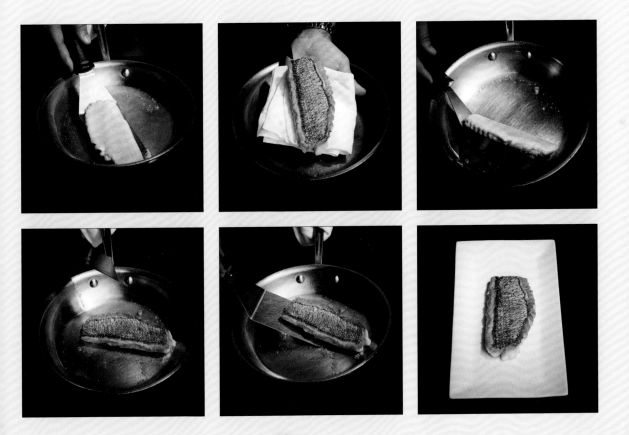

SMOKED SALMON "CROQUE-MONSIEUR"

SERVES 4

This recipe is an homage to my grandmother, who would often make traditional croque-monsieur (with ham). The challenge with this version is striking the right balance: You want the toast to have a nice color and crunchy texture and the cheese to melt just enough while keeping the salmon barely warm. If the salmon is overcooked, it will turn white and taste extremely salty. To make it extra luxurious, you can add caviar inside the sandwich, layered on the salmon, as we do at Le Bernardin.

6 ounces Gruyère cheese

8 slices (½ inch thick) Pullman bread or good-quality white sandwich bread

8 ounces smoked salmon, sliced ¼ inch thick

2 teaspoons thinly sliced fresh chives

6 tablespoons unsalted butter, at room temperature

SPECIAL EQUIPMENT

Mandoline

1. Using a Japanese mandoline or vegetable peeler, very thinly slice the Gruyère cheese.

2. Place 4 slices of the bread on the counter and cover with half the Gruyère. Divide the smoked salmon slices among the bread and sprinkle with the chives. Cover the salmon with the remaining Gruyère and top with the remaining bread slices. Using a serrated knife, cut off the crusts. (You may make the recipe up to this point 2 hours in advance. Cover with plastic wrap and refrigerate.)

3. Preheat a nonstick skillet over medium-high heat. Spread the softened butter on the outsides of the sandwiches. Add the sandwiches to the pan, in batches if needed, and cook without moving for 1 to 2 minutes. Flip them over and cook until the bread is golden and the cheese starts melting, but the salmon is not cooked, another 1 to 2 minutes.

4. To serve, slice the "croque-monsieur" in half diagonally, then on the diagonal again (you will have four triangles). Arrange the triangles on a plate. Serve immediately.

BRIOCHE-CRUSTED RED SNAPPER

SERVES 4

ANTICUCHO SAUCE

1 tablespoon canola oil

¼ cup thinly sliced shallot

2 garlic cloves, thinly sliced

1 tablespoon cumin seeds

2 cups thinly sliced yellow bell pepper, seeds removed

1 tablespoon ají amarillo pepper paste

4 sprigs cilantro

Fine sea salt and freshly ground white pepper

Juice of ½ lime

SNAPPER

1 loaf unsliced brioche, pain de mie, or good-quality white bread

4 pieces (7 ounces each) red snapper fillet, skinned

Fine sea salt and freshly ground white pepper

Extra-virgin olive oil

SPECIAL EQUIPMENT

Metal skewer

This dish is inspired by the street-food stalls of Peru where anticuchos—grilled skewers of different meats and offal—are marinated in a sauce using ají amarillo chiles. Brioche creates a nice crust, but you can use another white bread; just make sure that the bread is crunchy and the fish is moist.

1. Make the anticucho sauce: In a medium saucepan, heat the canola oil over medium heat. Add the shallot and garlic and cook until soft and golden, 3 to 4 minutes. Add the cumin and cook until fragrant and toasted, about 30 seconds. Add the bell pepper and cook until starting to soften, 4 to 5 minutes. Stir in the ají amarillo paste and about ½ cup water; the water should not cover the bell pepper. Bring to a simmer and cook for 5 minutes.

2. Transfer to a blender and process the sauce until smooth. If the sauce is too thick, stir in a tablespoon or two of warm water, then strain it through a fine-mesh sieve into a bowl.

3. Steep the cilantro in the sauce for 2 minutes, then remove and discard it. Season to taste with sea salt and white pepper and finish with the lime juice. Set aside and keep warm.

4. Prepare the snapper: Preheat the oven to 375°F. Put the bread in the freezer for 10 minutes to firm it up. Using a long serrated bread knife, cut off 4 long slices of bread, ⅛ to ¼ inch thick and the length of the fillet.

5. Season the snapper on both sides with sea salt and white pepper, then lay a fillet on each bread slice. Use a knife to trim off any overhang from the bread and discard it.

6. In each of two large nonstick ovenproof sauté pans, heat ¼ inch olive oil over medium heat. Add the snapper to the pans, bread side down. Gently cook, rotating the fish to evenly brown the bread, until golden brown, 2 to 3 minutes. Flip the fish over with a spatula and transfer the pans to the oven. Bake until a metal skewer inserted into the thickest part of the fish for 5 seconds feels warm when touched to your wrist, another 3 to 4 minutes.

7. Transfer to warm plates and serve with the anticucho sauce.

CRISPY BLACK BASS BASQUAISE

SERVES 4

Very often, fresh black bass can shrink when sautéed skin side down in the pan, so I recommend using a spatula to flatten the fish gently (be careful not to break the flesh) to ensure that it cooks evenly. You can also score the skin before placing in the pan to keep the fish from contracting too much. With that said, black bass is a great fish to sauté as the skin is thin and quite flavorful. It also doesn't have the layer of blood between flesh and skin (as found in other fish such as snapper or striped bass) that can give off a "fishy" taste.

1. In a medium saucepan, combine both bell peppers, the olive oil, and the garlic clove and lightly season with sea salt and white pepper. Place over medium heat and cook, making sure not to brown, until tender and fragrant, 12 to 15 minutes. Remove from the heat and set aside. Discard the garlic clove.

2. Season the black bass on both sides with sea salt and white pepper. Let the fish rest for 20 minutes. Pat the skin sides of the fish dry, then dust the skin sides only with Wondra flour.

3. Line a plate with paper towels and set it nearby. Set a nonstick medium skillet over high heat until very hot, but not smoking. Add 2 tablespoons of the canola oil, then 2 black bass fillets, skin sides down. Briefly press down on each fillet with a metal spatula to prevent the fish's skin from shrinking. Reduce the heat slightly and continue to press the fish flat. Once flattened, cook the fish until the skin is golden brown and crisp, 3 to 5 minutes. Flip the fish and cook until a metal skewer inserted into the thickest part of the fish for 5 seconds feels warm when touched to your wrist, about 1 minute. Transfer the fish to the paper towels to drain. Repeat with the remaining fillets and 2 tablespoons oil. (Alternatively, cook the fish simultaneously in two pans.)

4. Warm the peppers, then spoon them onto four warm plates. Top with the black bass and serve immediately.

1½ cups ¼-inch-diced red bell pepper

1½ cups ¼-inch-diced yellow bell pepper

½ cup extra-virgin olive oil

1 garlic clove, peeled

Fine sea salt and freshly ground white pepper

4 skin-on black bass fillets (7 ounces each)

Wondra flour

4 tablespoons canola oil

SPECIAL EQUIPMENT
Metal skewer

BLACKENED RED SNAPPER

SERVES 4

RED BEANS AND RICE

1¼ cups dried red beans

2 tablespoons extra-virgin olive oil

1 medium yellow onion, finely diced

2 garlic cloves, finely chopped

1½ teaspoons hot sauce

1 teaspoon dried oregano

Fine sea salt and freshly ground white pepper

1 cup long-grain white rice

BLACKENING SEASONING

2 tablespoons paprika

1 tablespoon dried basil

1 tablespoon dried oregano

1 tablespoon dried thyme

2 to 3 teaspoons cayenne pepper

1 teaspoon freshly ground black pepper

SNAPPER

4 red snapper fillets (7 ounces each), skinned

Fine sea salt

Canola oil

SPECIAL EQUIPMENT

Metal skewer

I ate blackened fish for the first time on a trip to Louisiana, and despite how it looks, it's not burned, nor do the dark color, crunchy texture, and spicy flavors overwhelm the fish. When your fish is moist and juicy and has a blackened, delicate crust, you know you have succeeded.

1. Prepare the red beans and rice: Put the red beans in a bowl and cover with water. Let soak overnight in the fridge. Drain the beans and discard the water. (Alternatively, you can use 3¾ cups high-quality canned red beans, drained.)

2. In a large heavy-bottomed pot, heat the olive oil over medium heat. Add the onion and cook for 2 to 3 minutes, till softened but not brown. Add the garlic and cook, making sure it doesn't brown, 2 to 3 minutes more.

3. Add the drained beans, hot sauce, oregano, and enough water to cover the beans by 2 inches. Bring to a simmer and cook, stirring every 20 minutes and adding water as needed to keep the beans soupy, until the beans are tender, about 1 hour. Season to taste with sea salt and white pepper.

4. While the beans are cooking, place the rice in a bowl and cover with cold water. Let stand for 5 minutes, then drain in a fine-mesh sieve. Rinse the rice until the water runs clear.

5. In a medium saucepan, bring 1½ cups water to a boil. Stir in the rice and 1 teaspoon fine sea salt, return to a simmer, cover, reduce the heat to low, and simmer for 15 minutes. Remove from the heat and steam the rice, covered, for 5 minutes, then uncover and fluff the rice. Set aside and keep warm.

6. Make the blackening seasoning: In a small bowl, combine the paprika, basil, oregano, thyme, cayenne, and black pepper. Mix well.

Recipe continues

7. Prepare the snapper: Season the fish lightly with sea salt, then generously coat it with the seasoning mixture. Dust off any excess and set aside.

8. Place a cast-iron skillet or heavy-bottomed sauté pan over high heat. Add just enough canola oil to coat the bottom of the pan. When the oil is very hot, add the snapper fillets without crowding (use two pans if needed) and cook for 2 minutes, until the bottom is charred. Flip and cook until a metal skewer inserted into the thickest part of the fish for 5 seconds feels warm when touched to your wrist, about 2 more minutes.

9. Remove from the pan and serve with the red beans and rice.

MONKFISH
WITH CABBAGE AND BACON BUTTER
SERVES 4

This is a throwback to the early days of Le Bernardin, where it was a signature dish of chef and owner Gilbert Le Coze. Monkfish is sometimes called the poor man's lobster as they have a similar texture, although monkfish is more tender. I suggest you use two pans so as not to overcrowd the fish and to produce a good crust. For serving, use a sharp knife to slice the cooked monkfish starting on the soft, noncrusted side to keep the crust on the individual slices intact.

1 head Savoy cabbage

Fine sea salt

5 ounces double-smoked slab bacon, cut into ½-inch cubes

4 sticks (1 pound) cold unsalted butter, cut into ½-inch pieces

Freshly ground white pepper

2 pounds cleaned monkfish tail, cut into 4 portions (8 ounces each), at room temperature

Wondra flour

Canola oil

SPECIAL EQUIPMENT

Metal skewer

1. Core the cabbage, remove 4 very green outer leaves, and set them aside. Pull off the light green leaves of the cabbage, saving the inner portion for another use. Cut the center rib out of each of the light green cabbage leaves. Stack the leaves, roll them up tightly, and cut the roll crosswise into ¼-inch-wide slices.

2. Bring a medium pot of water to a boil and season with sea salt. Fill a bowl with ice water. Blanch the 4 reserved outer cabbage leaves until crisp-tender, about 3 minutes. Transfer the leaves to the ice bath until cool, then remove and drain on a towel. Set aside.

3. In the same pot, blanch the sliced cabbage leaves until fully tender, 2 to 3 minutes. Transfer the leaves to the ice bath until cool, then drain and set aside.

4. Preheat the oven to 450°F.

5. In a medium saucepan, sauté the bacon over medium heat until golden and crisp, 3 to 4 minutes. Drain off the fat. Return the pan of bacon to medium heat, add 2 tablespoons water, and scrape up any caramelized bits with a wooden spoon. Once the liquid returns to a simmer, add one-quarter of the butter at a time, whisking constantly, until all the butter is incorporated. Season with sea salt and white pepper to taste. Strain through a fine-mesh sieve into a small saucepan, set aside, and keep warm. Eat the bacon or save it for another use.

Recipe continues

6. Season the monkfish with sea salt and white pepper. Lightly dust the flat side of each monkfish fillet with Wondra flour, shaking off the excess. Place two large ovenproof sauté pans over medium-high heat and add enough canola oil to just coat the pans. Put 2 pieces of monkfish in each pan, flour side down, and sauté without moving until browned on the bottom, about 5 minutes. Adjust the heat if needed to form a nice crust without burning.

7. Transfer the pans to the oven without turning the fish. Roast the fish for 5 minutes, then turn the fish and cook until a metal skewer inserted into the thickest part of the fish for 5 seconds feels warm when touched to your wrist, about 1 minute longer. Transfer the fish to a cutting board crust side up and let rest for 4 to 5 minutes before slicing.

8. While the fish is resting, put the sliced cabbage in a saucepan along with ½ cup of the bacon butter. Place it over medium heat until hot. Season with sea salt and white pepper.

9. Place one of the 4 whole cabbage leaves in the center of each warmed plate and top with one-quarter of the sliced warmed cabbage, making it into an oval-shaped bed for the fish. Starting on the uncrusted side of the monkfish, cut it crosswise into ¼-inch-wide slices and season with sea salt and white pepper. Fan the monkfish slices crust side up over the cabbage. Spoon bacon butter over the fish and around the cabbage to cover the plates. Serve immediately. Keep any extra sauce at the table, as it's so good people will surely want more!

CALAMARI "TAGLIATELLE"

SERVES 6

2 pounds medium calamari tubes, rinsed

2 tablespoons canola oil

2 garlic cloves, peeled

¼ cup finely diced red bell pepper

Fine sea salt and freshly ground white pepper

Pinch of cayenne pepper

2 tablespoons chopped fresh flat-leaf parsley

1 lemon, halved and seeded

If you can't find fresh calamari, good-quality frozen calamari are often readily available at the store. If you do manage to find the fresh kind, they should be already cleaned by the fishmonger and very white in color—if they have a reddish or pinkish hue, they are already old. To keep calamari tender, they must be sautéed quickly; the longer they are cooked, the tougher their texture becomes. Drizzle any leftover cooking juices onto each plate before serving.

1. Lay a calamari tube on a cutting board with the round opening facing you. Insert the tip of the knife and cut lengthwise through one side of the tube, then open it like a book to form a flat sheet. Repeat with the rest of the calamari. Cut the calamari sheets into 2 × ½-inch strips. Set aside and keep cold.

2. In a large nonstick sauté pan, combine the canola oil and garlic cloves and set over medium-high heat. When the garlic begins to sizzle and is well browned, remove it from the pan and discard. Add the diced red pepper and cook for 1 minute.

3. Add the calamari and cook, tossing frequently for even cooking, for 1 to 2 minutes to your desired doneness. Season with sea salt, white pepper, and the cayenne. Add the parsley and toss to combine. Remove from the heat. Taste and adjust the seasoning with sea salt and white pepper if necessary.

4. Divide the calamari among six dishes, squeeze a little lemon juice over the top, and serve immediately.

TUNA NIÇOISE

SERVES 2

This is a hat-tip to the salade niçoise, though we are using fresh tuna here, not canned tuna as in the classic recipe. Charring the tuna on one side gives it a great smoky flavor, though take care to char it quickly and remove from the heat, as the fish will continue to cook. It should be served warm, rare to medium-rare. You can reduce or increase the garnish to your taste.

1. Make the vinaigrette: In a small bowl, whisk together the vinegar, mustard, sea salt, and white pepper until the salt dissolves. Constantly whisking, slowly drizzle in the olive oil.

2. Prepare the salad components: Bring a small pot of water to a boil. Set up two bowls filled with ice water. Place the egg in the pot of boiling water and simmer for 6 minutes. Remove with a slotted spoon, keeping the water at a boil, and cool the egg under cold running water. When cool enough to handle, crack and peel the shell. Set the peeled egg aside.

3. Season the boiling water with sea salt. Blanch the haricots verts until crisp-tender, about 5 minutes. Transfer the beans to one bowl of ice water. Once cool, drain the beans on a kitchen towel and set aside.

4. Shave the fennel lengthwise on a mandoline. Place the fennel in the other bowl of ice water until the slices crisp and curl up. Drain on a kitchen towel and set aside.

5. Place the haricots verts, shaved fennel, olives, tomatoes, bell pepper, and celery in a bowl and season with sea salt and white pepper. Toss the vegetables with enough vinaigrette to coat. Cut the egg into quarters and set aside.

6. Cook the tuna: Heat a cast-iron skillet or large heavy-bottomed sauté pan until it is very hot. Season the tuna with sea salt and white

Recipe continues

VINAIGRETTE

3 tablespoons sherry vinegar

1 teaspoon Dijon mustard

½ teaspoon fine sea salt

Pinch of freshly ground white pepper

½ cup extra-virgin olive oil

SALAD

1 large egg, at room temperature

Fine sea salt

¼ pound haricots verts, trimmed

1 medium fennel bulb, top cut off and discarded

10 niçoise olives, pitted and quartered

4 red cherry tomatoes, quartered

4 yellow cherry tomatoes, quartered

½ red bell pepper, thinly sliced

1 rib celery, cut on the diagonal into ¼-inch-thick slices

Freshly ground white pepper

TUNA

2 tuna steaks (8 ounces each), about 4 × 3½ inches and 1 inch thick, at room temperature

Fine sea salt and freshly ground white pepper

2 teaspoons canola oil

2 tablespoons extra-virgin olive oil

TO FINISH

1 lemon, halved and seeded

½ cup baby arugula or
mesclun greens

SPECIAL EQUIPMENT

Mandoline

Pastry brush

pepper on both sides. With a pastry brush, paint the tuna on one side with the canola oil. Place the tuna in the pan, oiled side down, and sear until nicely browned but still rare, about 1 minute. Remove from the pan.

7. Brush the rare (unseared) sides of the tuna with the olive oil. Place a tuna steak, rare side up, in the center of each plate.

8. To finish: Squeeze lemon juice over the tuna. Add the arugula to the bowl with the vegetables and toss to combine, adding a little more dressing. Taste and adjust the seasoning if necessary.

9. Divide the salad evenly and mound it on top of each piece of tuna. Add the eggs alongside and serve immediately. Store any leftover dressing in an airtight container in the refrigerator for up to 3 days.

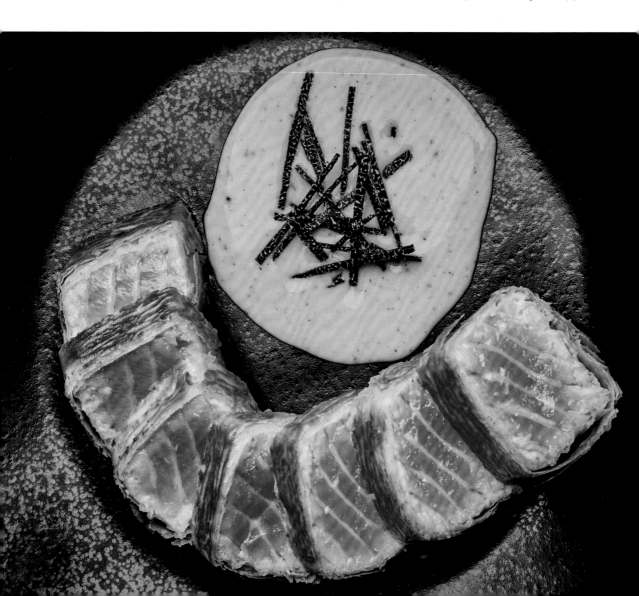

SALMON STRUDEL

SERVES 4

To achieve a light crispy, flaky phyllo crust, wrap the salmon in the phyllo neatly, but leave just enough room for the dough to create layers. If you wrap the fish too tightly, it will prevent the phyllo from becoming crunchy and will render the pastry soft and soggy. This is an easy recipe once you learn to work fast, and while it's designed to serve four, you may want to halve the recipe and try it for two the first time you make it.

1. Wrap the salmon: Season the salmon fillets with sea salt and white pepper on all sides.

2. Using a pastry brush, paint the top of one sheet of phyllo with some melted butter. Top with a second phyllo sheet and brush with butter. Repeat twice more for a total of 4 buttered phyllo sheets. Fold the pile in half to make a 12 × 6-inch rectangle. Brush the top with butter again. Center a salmon fillet crosswise at a short end of the rectangle, then roll it up in the phyllo dough to enclose; the ends can remain open. Repeat with the remaining phyllo and salmon.

3. Make the truffle butter: In a small saucepan, bring the truffle juice to a boil, then reduce to a simmer and cook until reduced to 3 to 4 tablespoons, about 7 minutes. Whisk in the butter, a bit at a time, until it is fully incorporated. Stir in the chopped truffles. Remove from the heat, season with salt and white pepper, and set aside until ready to serve.

4. To finish: Divide the canola oil between two large nonstick pans and heat over medium heat. Add 2 salmon-phyllo packets to each pan and cook until golden brown on both sides, about 16 minutes total. Reduce the heat to medium-low if the phyllo browns too quickly. A metal skewer inserted into the thickest part of the fish for 5 seconds should feel warm when touched to your wrist.

5. Using a serrated knife, trim the ends off each salmon-phyllo bundle, then gently slice each into 6 or 7 slices. Fan the slices onto warm plates and finish with warm truffle butter and julienne of truffles for garnish. Serve immediately.

SALMON

1½-pound center-cut salmon fillet, skinned and pin bones removed, cut into four 4 × 2-inch rectangles 2 inches thick

Fine sea salt and freshly ground white pepper

16 sheets phyllo dough, cut to 12 ×12 inches

6 tablespoons unsalted butter, melted

TRUFFLE BUTTER

⅔ cup truffle juice

1 stick (4 ounces) unsalted butter, cut into small pieces

½ ounce finely chopped black truffles

Fine sea salt and freshly ground white pepper

TO FINISH

3 tablespoons canola oil

Finely julienned fresh black truffle for garnish

SPECIAL EQUIPMENT

Pastry brush

Metal skewer

7
BROILED

BROIL

To cook directly under a heat source

B roiling is similar to grilling except the heat source comes from above rather than underneath. You don't get the same charred effects as you do from grilling, but you can achieve a nice, even color on your fish. Broiling is an effective way to sear seafood quickly without overcooking it, and depending on the size of your broiler, it allows you to cook for a crowd. A broiler is also good for flash-warming a dish very quickly, such as the Scallops and Chives with Nage (page 220), and for giving certain dishes a good color, such as the Crab Gratin (page 216).

BROILING

1. Preheat the broiler to high (500°F) for 10 minutes.

2. Pat the fish dry to remove any excess moisture, then season with fine sea salt and freshly ground white pepper.

3. With a pastry brush, lightly coat a broiler-proof sheet pan with a small amount of neutral oil, like canola oil or vegetable oil.

4. Place the fish on the sheet pan, then brush the fish lightly with the neutral oil.

5. Place under the broiler about 2 inches from the heat source for every ½-inch thickness. So, for example, a fish 1 inch thick should be about 4 inches from the heat. Cook for 2 minutes per every ½ inch of the fish's thickness or to the desired doneness. A metal skewer inserted into the thickest part of the fish for 5 seconds should feel warm when touched to your wrist.

LOBSTER THERMIDOR

SERVES 4

4 live Maine lobsters
(1¾ pounds each)

Fine sea salt

6 tablespoons unsalted butter,
at room temperature

2 tablespoons minced onion

1 tablespoon all-purpose flour

¼ cup Cognac or other brandy

½ cup whole milk

2 tablespoons crème fraîche

1½ tablespoons fresh tarragon,
finely chopped

½ teaspoon spicy dry mustard
(optional)

¼ teaspoon cayenne pepper
(optional)

Freshly ground white pepper

1½ tablespoons bread crumbs

Paprika

SPECIAL EQUIPMENT

Pastry brush

This dish is a timeless classic. Even though it's already quite rich, I like it slightly spicier than normal, so I try to use the spiciest mustard I can find, or cayenne pepper. As with any other type of seafood, always take care not to overcook the lobster, as it will become chewy and flavorless.

1. Preheat the broiler to high (500°F). Bring a large pot of water to a boil.

2. Place a lobster belly down on a cutting board, then place the tip of a sharp knife in the center of the head with the blade pointing toward the front of the head. Press down, splitting the head in two; this will kill the lobster quickly. (See How to Split a Lobster, page 12, for photos.)

3. Remove the rubber bands from the lobster's claws with the tip of your knife. Turn the lobster over and remove the front knuckles and claws by twisting them off the base of the body. Set aside.

4. Return the lobster to the cutting board, belly side facing up. Starting from where the head meets the tail, cut 90 percent of the way through the body, leaving the outer shell intact, and continuing through the tail. Turn the lobster 180 degrees and continue cutting through the head. Repeat with the remaining lobsters.

5. When the water reaches a boil, season it with sea salt, then add the claws, lower the heat, and cook at a simmer for 5 minutes. Remove and let cool.

6. Holding each lobster in your hands, open it like a book to expose the flesh and tomalley, the green substance found near the head. Gently clean the inside of the head section into a bowl.

Recipe continues

7. Place the lobsters on a sheet pan, flesh side up, and use a pastry brush to coat each with 1 tablespoon of the softened butter. Broil 4 inches from the heat for 90 seconds, or until the meat can be pulled from the shells. Leave the broiler on.

8. Remove the meat from the lobster shells. Set the shells aside. Next, crack the claws and remove the meat, discarding any cartilage or claw shells.

9. Roughly chop all the lobster meat into ½-inch chunks, place it in a large bowl, and set aside.

10. In a skillet, melt the remaining 2 tablespoons butter over medium heat. Add the onion and a pinch of sea salt. Add the flour and cook until well combined, about 2 minutes. Remove from the heat and carefully add the Cognac, return to the burner, and cook until reduced by half, about 2 minutes. Add the milk and bring to a simmer, cooking until thickened, another 2 to 3 minutes. Remove from the heat and allow to cool.

11. When the sauce has cooled, add it to the bowl with the chopped lobster meat, along with the crème fraîche, tarragon, and mustard and/or cayenne (if using). Season lightly with sea salt and white pepper and stir until well combined. Divide the mixture evenly among the cleaned and reserved lobster shells. Sprinkle with bread crumbs and paprika.

12. Line a sheet pan with crumpled foil to hold the lobsters in place. Place the filled lobster halves on the sheet pan and transfer to the broiler. Broil 4 inches from the heat until lightly browned and bubbling, 3 to 4 minutes. Transfer to plates and serve immediately.

OYSTERS AND CLAMS
WITH "SNAIL BUTTER"

SERVES 4

Inspired by the technique used in France for preparing escargots, aka snails, I recommend using large, deep-shelled oysters as they contain more juice. For the clams, topnecks—a size between littlenecks and cherrystones—work best. Serve warm with good bread on the side.

4 cups kosher salt

12 tablespoons (1½ sticks) unsalted butter, at room temperature

1 garlic clove, finely minced

2 tablespoons chopped fresh flat-leaf parsley

2 teaspoons fresh lemon juice

Fine sea salt and freshly ground white pepper

12 oysters

12 topneck clams

12 sprigs thyme

1. Preheat the broiler to high (500°F).

2. In a large bowl, mix 2 cups of the kosher salt with just enough water to make it the consistency of wet sand and set aside. Pour the remaining 2 cups kosher salt on a sheet pan.

3. In a small bowl, stir the softened butter until creamy. Add the garlic, parsley, and lemon juice and stir until well mixed. Season with sea salt and white pepper and set aside.

4. To prepare the oysters for cooking (see How to Shuck an Oyster, page 14, for photos), start by placing a kitchen towel on a table in front of you. Fold the towel in half lengthwise and then in half again, giving you a pocket to hold the oyster.

5. Place an oyster, belly side (rounded side) down, in the fold with the hinge (the pointed back end) facing out.

6. Using your nondominant hand, firmly put pressure on top of the towel to hold the oyster in place.

7. With your dominant hand, place the tip of an oyster knife into the oyster's hinge and slowly wiggle the knife to find the separation point to break the ligament that keeps the two shells together. You will feel a small pop when the shells detach.

8. Once shells are detached, twist the knife handle so that the handle now points toward you and slide the tip of the knife under the top side of the shell. This will detach the adductor muscle so you can remove the top shell.

Recipe continues

9. Gently slide the tip of the knife underneath the oyster to detach the adductor muscle from the bottom shell, while keeping the oyster sitting inside the bottom shell. Check for pieces of shell or debris and remove them. Smell the oyster for freshness and discard any oyster that smells off.

10. To prepare the clams for cooking (see How to Shuck a Clam, page 16, for photos), first wash them thoroughly in cold water.

11. Using a towel or glove, hold the clam in your nondominant hand with the hinge tucked in toward your palm where it meets the thumb. Insert the tip of a clam knife or paring knife between the top and bottom shells. Cut around the front lip of the clam, between the two halves of the shell, then twist to pry it open.

12. With the tip of the knife, disconnect the clam meat from the top shell. Use the tip of the knife to twist off the top shell. Disconnect the meat from the bottom shell using the tip of the knife, but keep the clam sitting in the bottom shell.

13. Spoon ½ tablespoon of the garlic butter on top of each oyster and clam. Place them on the salt-covered sheet pan and refrigerate.

14. Prepare 4 appetizer-sized plates by placing one-quarter of the wet salt mixture on each. This will serve as a bed for the cooked oysters and clams.

15. Remove the sheet pan from the refrigerator and place ½ sprig thyme over each oyster and clam. Place the pan of oysters and clams under the broiler, 4 inches from the heat, until the butter is bubbling, 2 to 3 minutes.

16. Discard the thyme and transfer 3 oysters and 3 clams to each plate. Serve immediately.

WARM SALMON CARPACCIO

SERVES 4

1 tablespoon drained capers

6 tablespoons extra-virgin olive oil

4 sushi-quality salmon pieces (4 ounces each)

Fine sea salt and freshly ground white pepper

1 tablespoon fresh dill leaves

1 lemon, halved and seeded

Toasted baguette slices for serving

SPECIAL EQUIPMENT

Flat meat pounder

Wide pastry brush

If you don't want to go through the process of pounding the salmon for carpaccio (see page 24), you can slice it into ¼-inch-thick slices instead—just be sure to cut enough to cover the plate completely. Either way, the dish should be served immediately after warming the plate, as it will continue to cook the fish, which should still be almost raw.

1. Dry the capers on a paper towel.

2. In a skillet, heat 2 tablespoons of the olive oil over medium-high heat. Add the capers and fry until crispy, about 2 minutes. Transfer to a paper towel to drain and set aside.

3. Cover your work surface, such as a counter or table, with a large sheet of plastic wrap. Place 4 ounces of sliced salmon side by side in the center of the plastic wrap and cover with another large sheet of plastic. (See pages 24 and 25 for photos.)

4. Flatten the salmon with a meat pounder (or a heavy-bottomed saucepan), using a fluid motion that combines hitting the salmon in the center and sliding the surface of the pounder over the salmon, pressing it outward. Continue pounding and pressing out the salmon until there is a very thin, even round, about 9 inches in diameter.

5. Place an 8-inch plate, bowl, or cake pan to use as a cutting guide over the salmon (the salmon should still be covered with plastic) and use a sharp knife to cut through the salmon and both layers of plastic, resulting in an 8-inch round of salmon. Leave the plastic on the salmon. Repeat with the remaining 3 portions of salmon.

6. Place the salmon rounds on a sheet pan and refrigerate for 30 minutes. (The salmon can be pounded and cut up to a few hours ahead; cover the entire pan with plastic and refrigerate.)

7. Preheat the broiler to medium (450°F).

Recipe continues

8. When ready to serve, pull the top plastic sheet off one salmon round. Place the salmon (plastic side up) in the center of a large dinner plate. Pull the plastic sheet off the top of the salmon. Repeat with the remaining salmon rounds. Season each piece with sea salt and white pepper. Dip the pastry brush in the remaining olive oil and coat each salmon round with a small amount of extra-virgin olive oil.

9. Place each plate of salmon carpaccio quickly under the broiler, 6 inches from the heat, for 10 to 15 seconds, just until it begins to change color.

10. Garnish with the fried capers and dill leaves, then squeeze lemon juice over the salmon. Serve immediately, passing the toasts on a separate plate.

MISO COD "NOBU"

SERVES 4

It's difficult to present a miso cod recipe and not salute the great Nobu Matsuhisa, who made this dish popular in America. You can also use other fish that are rich, oily, and flaky, such as Chilean sea bass. This dish is consistently delicious and so simple, it's almost idiotproof! Merci, Nobu-san!

1. Make the wasabi-lime dressing: In a blender, combine the wasabi, lime juice, and lemon juice and process. With the machine running, slowly emulsify in the ginger oil and then the canola oil. Add sugar and season with sea salt and white pepper to taste. Place in an airtight container and keep refrigerated.

2. Marinate the cod: In a medium saucepan, combine the sake and mirin and bring to a boil over medium-high heat. Reduce the heat slightly, then add the miso and sugar a little at a time, stirring to fully incorporate them into a smooth paste. Remove from the heat and let cool to room temperature.

3. Pour the marinade into the bottom of a baking dish large enough to hold all of the fillets of fish. Place the cod in the miso and stir to completely cover. Cover and refrigerate for 2 to 3 days.

4. When ready to cook, preheat the broiler to low (400°F).

5. Remove the cod from the miso and scrape off any excess marinade. Lightly oil a sheet pan with a little bit of canola oil or cooking spray. Arrange the fish on the sheet pan.

6. Put the sheet pan in the oven 4 to 6 inches from the heat source and broil the marinated cod until evenly browned and a metal skewer inserted into the thickest part of the fish for 5 seconds feels warm when touched to your wrist, 3 to 4 minutes.

7. Transfer the cod to warm plates and serve immediately with the wasabi-lime dressing alongside.

Recipe continues

WASABI-LIME DRESSING

2 teaspoons wasabi paste

3 tablespoons fresh lime juice

1 tablespoon fresh lemon juice

1½ tablespoons Ginger Oil (page 211)

5 tablespoons canola oil

¼ teaspoon sugar

Fine sea salt and freshly ground white pepper

COD

½ cup Japanese sake

½ cup mirin

1 cup white miso paste

3 tablespoons sugar

4 skin-on black cod fillets (7 ounces each)

Canola oil or cooking spray for the pan

SPECIAL EQUIPMENT

Metal skewer

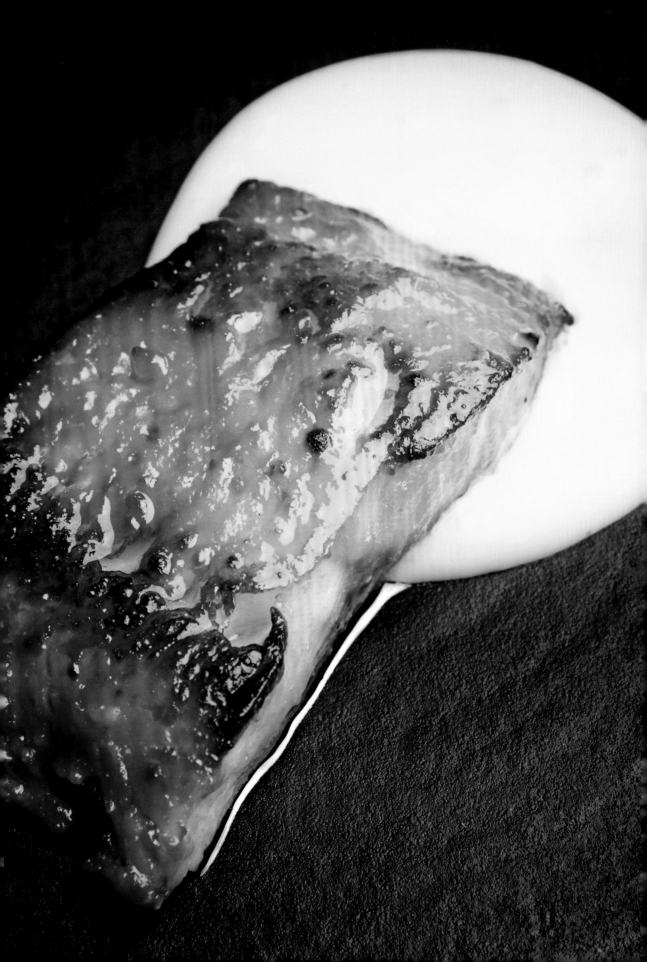

GINGER OIL

1. Put the ginger in a blender and blend in the oil at high speed.

2. Remove the oil to a clean container and seal tightly. Let stand at room temperature at least 2 hours, or refrigerate overnight, before using. The ginger oil will keep in the refrigerator for up to 2 weeks.

½ pound fresh ginger, peeled and minced

1 cup canola oil

SHRIMP, SWEET GARLIC, AND EXTRA-VIRGIN OLIVE OIL

SERVES 4

24 extra large shrimp (26/30 count), peeled and deveined

Fine sea salt and freshly ground white pepper

2 garlic cloves, thinly sliced

⅔ cup extra-virgin olive oil

2 tablespoons chopped parsley

1 teaspoon paprika

This recipe is a true and simple nod to Spanish cuisine. I like the shrimp cooked but still slightly translucent. At the last second, I add chopped parsley and paprika. The oil is delicious when soaked up with crusty bread.

1. Preheat the broiler to medium (450°F).

2. Season the shrimp with sea salt and white pepper, then place in a broiler-safe baking dish just large enough to hold all the shrimp in a single layer.

3. In a small saucepan, combine the garlic and oil and bring to a simmer. Pour over the shrimp.

4. Place the baking dish in the broiler 4 inches from the heat source and broil until the shrimp are just opaque, 2 to 3 minutes. Remove and let rest for 2 to 3 minutes. Add parsley and paprika, and serve hot.

MONKFISH "BYALDI"

SERVES 4

Monkfish has a great meatiness to it that works nicely in this recipe; however, striped bass, red snapper, or any other white fish is a good substitute. A byaldi is a more refined style of ratatouille, where the vegetables are thinly sliced and layered over a bed of caramelized onions. The vegetables and chorizo protect the fish from the heat of the oven, while their juices keep it moist and add tons of flavor. When serving, slice between the layers with a very sharp knife for a nice, clean cut.

1. To butterfly the monkfish, lay one loin on a cutting board with a short end facing you. Use your nondominant hand to hold the loin in place. With your dominant hand, place a sharp knife against the right side of the loin, making sure the loin is centered against the blade of the knife. Cut three-quarters of the way toward the left side, then open the flesh like a book. Repeat with remaining 3 loins and set aside.

2. Lightly coat a sheet pan with extra-virgin olive oil. Season the monkfish loins with sea salt and white pepper and evenly space them on the pan, short sides facing you.

3. Starting from the left-hand side of each monkfish loin, tightly layer zucchini half-moons the width of the loin, slightly overlapping the pieces. (You should use 3 or 4 pieces, depending on size, per row.) Continue with alternating rows of yellow squash, chorizo, tomato, and mushroom until the fish is covered. Season with sea salt, white pepper, and the herbes de Provence. Set aside and keep cool until ready to cook.

4. Preheat the broiler to low (400°F).

5. When ready to cook, drizzle extra-virgin olive oil over the vegetables and place the sheet pan under the broiler 6 inches from the heat. Cook until the vegetables are golden brown and the chorizo begins to curl, about 5 minutes. A metal skewer inserted into the thickest part of the fish for 5 seconds should feel warm when touched to your wrist.

6. Remove from the broiler and let rest for 4 to 5 minutes. Using a spatula, transfer to warm plates, spoon any cooking liquid from the tray over each loin, and serve immediately.

4 monkfish loins
(7 ounces each)

Extra-virgin olive oil

Fine sea salt and freshly ground white pepper

2 cups ¼-inch-thick half-moons zucchini

2 cups ¼-inch-thick half-moons yellow squash

2 cups ¼-inch-thick half-moons cured chorizo

2 cups ¼-inch-thick half-moons plum tomato

2 cups ¼-inch-thick slices large white mushroom

1½ teaspoons herbes de Provence

SPECIAL EQUIPMENT

Metal skewer

CRAB GRATIN

SERVES 4

2 tablespoons unsalted butter

2 tablespoons all-purpose flour

2 cups whole milk

1 tablespoon Dijon mustard

¼ teaspoon freshly grated nutmeg

Fine sea salt and freshly ground white pepper

1 pound fresh jumbo lump crabmeat, picked over to remove any bits of shell or cartilage

4 tablespoons dried bread crumbs

SPECIAL EQUIPMENT

12-inch gratin dish or 4 mini gratin dishes

Crab gratin will always be a time-honored, classic French comfort food dish. When I was growing up, my grandmother made this for me very often, and to this day I still serve it in a scallop shell, as she did. When cleaning the crab and removing any bits of shell and cartilage from the flesh, take care not to break the crab up too much in order to preserve its texture.

1. In a saucepan, melt the butter over medium heat. Add the flour a little at a time and stir well, about 1 minute. Whisk the milk in slowly until it is fully incorporated and lump-free. Whisk in the mustard, bring to a simmer, and cook until the sauce is thick enough to coat the back of a spoon, 4 to 5 minutes. Season the béchamel with the nutmeg and sea salt and white pepper to taste.

2. Preheat the broiler to medium (450°F).

3. Place the crab in a bowl and lightly season it with sea salt and white pepper. Spoon the béchamel over the crab and gently mix.

4. Place the crab and béchamel mixture in a 12-inch gratin dish (or divide it among 4 mini gratin dishes) and top with the bread crumbs. Place under the broiler 6 inches from the heat source and broil until golden brown and bubbling, about 2 minutes for mini gratin dishes or 3 minutes for a large dish. Remove and serve hot.

SEA BASS
WITH CHARRED LEMON VINAIGRETTE
SERVES 4

This is a very simple and versatile recipe, and the technique can be applied to any white fish. It's important that the lemon for the vinaigrette be charred to give it a special dimension. To make this dish even simpler, skip the second step and leave the skin on the potatoes.

1. Place the potatoes in a pot and add cold water to cover by 1 inch. Season with sea salt. Bring to a boil and cook until the potatoes are tender, 12 to 14 minutes. Drain.

2. When the potatoes are cool enough to handle, peel them with a paring knife. Put them in a bowl and gently stir in the chives. Cover and keep warm.

3. Heat a skillet over medium-high heat. Lightly oil the pan, then add the lemon halves, cut side down, and cook until charred, 4 to 5 minutes.

4. Squeeze the lemon juice into a bowl, discarding any seeds. Stir in the vinegar and a pinch of sea salt. Slowly drizzle in the extra-virgin olive oil, whisking until it emulsifies. Cover and set aside.

5. Heat a large skillet over medium-high heat and add olive oil to coat the bottom. Add the broccoli rabe, reduce the heat to medium, and season with sea salt. Sauté until the broccoli rabe is tender, 6 to 8 minutes. Stir in the pepper flakes and remove from the heat.

6. Preheat the broiler to low (400°F).

7. Season the sea bass fillets on both sides with sea salt and white pepper. Place on a sheet pan and use a pastry brush to lightly coat each fillet with canola oil. Place under the broiler about 4 inches from the heat source. Broil for 5 minutes and check for doneness by inserting a skewer in the thickest part of the fish for 5 seconds; it should be warm to the touch on your wrist.

8. Transfer the sea bass to warm plates. Plate the warm potatoes and broccoli rabe alongside, pour the charred lemon vinaigrette over and around the fish, and serve.

1 pound small Yukon Gold potatoes, washed

Fine sea salt

1 teaspoon finely sliced fresh chives

Canola oil for the skillet and for brushing

2 lemons, halved

1 tablespoon red wine vinegar

½ cup extra-virgin olive oil, plus more for sautéing

1 bunch broccoli rabe, florets trimmed and thick stems removed

½ teaspoon red pepper flakes

4 sea bass fillets (7 ounces each), skinned

Freshly ground white pepper

SPECIAL EQUIPMENT

Pastry brush

Metal skewer

SCALLOPS AND CHIVES WITH NAGE

SERVES 4

NAGE

¼ cup champagne vinegar

½ cup dry white wine

1 garlic clove, peeled

½ large onion, peeled
and halved

¼ medium carrot, peeled
and halved

1 rib celery, quartered

½ leek, cleaned and quartered

Fine sea salt and freshly
ground white pepper

SCALLOPS

3 tablespoons unsalted butter

8 large or 12 medium scallops

Pinch of cayenne pepper

Fine sea salt and freshly
ground white pepper

1 tablespoon thinly sliced
fresh chives

As elegant as it is simple, this dish is a wonderful way to prepare and serve scallops. Once you have cooked the nage, you can reuse the vegetables in other ways, such as adding them to a salad to brighten it up.

1. Make the nage: In a saucepan, combine the vinegar, wine, garlic, onion, carrot, celery, leek, and 2 cups cold water and bring to a simmer. Simmer until the liquid is reduced to 1 cup, about 1 hour. Strain and season with sea salt and white pepper. Set aside.

2. Cook the scallops: Lightly rub four ovenproof plates with 1 tablespoon of the butter. Slice the scallops horizontally into ¼-inch-thick disks and arrange them on the plates in a circular pattern.

3. Preheat the broiler to medium (450°F).

4. Bring the nage to a simmer and whisk in the remaining 2 tablespoons butter until fully incorporated. Set aside and keep warm.

5. Season the scallops with cayenne pepper, sea salt, and white pepper to taste. Slide the plates under the broiler 4 inches from the heat source and broil until just warm but not cooked through, 30 to 45 seconds.

6. Remove from the broiler and pour some of the hot nage over each plate, just enough to barely cover the scallop disks. Do not submerge the scallops. Sprinkle with the chives and serve immediately.

BBQ-GLAZED STRIPED BASS

SERVES 4

Because barbecue sauce is sweet and powerful in flavor, I suggest using a fish that is firm in texture and not too delicate in flavor. Cod, grouper, or even swordfish would stand up to the strong sauce just as well as striped bass does.

1. Make the coleslaw: In a large bowl, combine the cabbage, carrot, scallions, and tarragon and gently toss together. In a separate bowl, combine the mayonnaise, wine vinegar, granulated sugar, and sea salt and black pepper to taste. Stir or whisk until well combined. Pour the dressing over the cabbage and mix well. Taste a piece of cabbage and adjust the seasoning if necessary. Place in the refrigerator and let rest for at least 1 hour.

2. Prepare the bass: In a small bowl, whisk together the ketchup, cider vinegar, Worcestershire sauce, brown sugar, and mustard powder until well combined. Season with sea salt and white pepper. Set the BBQ sauce aside.

3. Preheat the broiler to medium (450°F).

4. Season the striped bass fillets on both sides with sea salt and white pepper. Place on a broiler pan or sheet pan. Place under the broiler and broil about 6 inches from the heat source for 2 minutes. Flip the fillets over and broil for another 2 minutes. Remove from the oven.

5. Using a spoon or a pastry brush, cover the striped bass with the BBQ sauce and return it to the broiler. Cook until the sauce starts to caramelize slightly and a skewer inserted into the thickest part of the fish for 5 seconds feels warm when touched to your wrist.

6. Transfer the fish to warm plates and serve with the coleslaw alongside.

COLESLAW

½ head green cabbage (about 1 pound), quartered, cored, and very thinly sliced

½ large carrot, grated

3 scallions, thinly sliced

1 tablespoon finely chopped fresh tarragon leaves

¼ cup mayonnaise

1½ tablespoons red wine vinegar

1 tablespoon granulated sugar

Fine sea salt and freshly ground black pepper

BBQ BASS

½ cup ketchup

1 tablespoon cider vinegar

1 tablespoon Worcestershire sauce

1 tablespoon light brown sugar

¼ teaspoon mustard powder

Fine sea salt and freshly ground white pepper

4 striped bass fillets (7 ounces each), skinned

SPECIAL EQUIPMENT

Pastry brush

Metal skewer

8

GRILLED

GRILL

To cook using a grill over a heat source

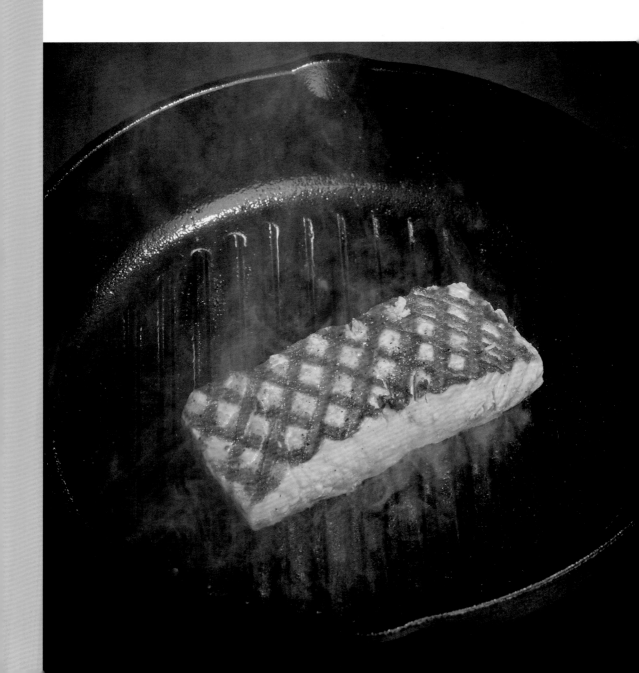

hough grilling and broiling are very similar techniques, there are some key differences: When broiling, the food cooks directly underneath the heat source, whereas when grilling, food is cooked on a metal grate directly over an open flame or in a ridged stovetop grill pan.

Grilling is a healthy way of cooking as it uses little or no fat, with the flavor coming directly from the smoky char of the grill itself, and it's usually a quick way to cook. An outdoor grill has the added benefit of keeping your kitchen cool during warmer weather.

Firm and fatty fish lend themselves well to grilling. This is a collection of my favorite dishes when I'm grilling outside and entertaining friends and family during the summer months, but most of them can also be cooked inside on a grill pan, as demonstrated here.

1. Preheat a grill pan on your stove over medium-high heat or preheat your outdoor grill to medium-high. (For the outdoor grill, make sure the grate is very clean.)

2. Remove any excess moisture from your fish by patting it dry with a paper towel, and season with fine sea salt and freshly ground white pepper.

3. Using a pastry brush, apply a small amount of canola oil to both sides of the fish.

4. When the grill pan or grill is hot, lightly brush the pan or grate with a neutral oil and carefully lay the fish on the pan/grill.

5. Let cook for 2 to 3 minutes without moving. Using a spatula, gently lift the fish and rotate it 90 degrees. If the fish is sticking when you try to turn it, let it cook for an additional minute and it should release.

6. As the fish cooks, brush a small amount of neutral oil over the top.

7. Gently turn the fish over to finish cooking to your desired doneness or until a metal skewer inserted into the thickest part of the fish for 5 seconds feels warm when touched to your wrist.

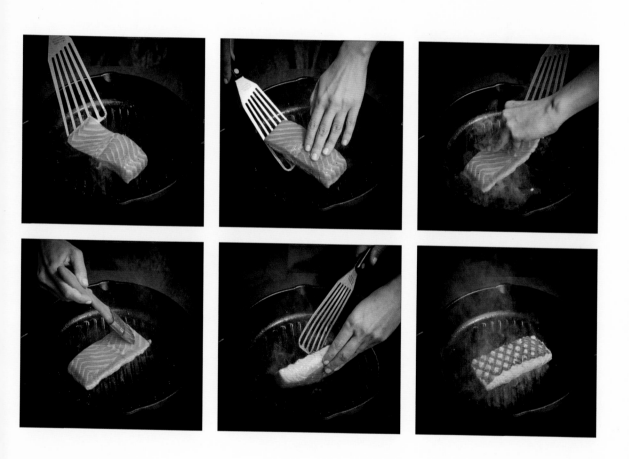

CHERRYSTONE CLAMS
WITH LEMON AND TABASCO
SERVES 4

Cherrystones become chewy and hard if overcooked, so monitor them closely. I like to grill the clams using charcoal or wood, which adds a smoky flavor. However, you could also follow this technique and broil the clams. Keep the juice in the shells when serving, but if you are drinking the juice directly from the shell, be aware of the shell's salty underside. Make sure to eat the clams immediately, when they're still hot.

24 cherrystone or littleneck clams

48-ounce box kosher salt

Lemon wedges for serving

Tabasco or other hot sauce for serving

SPECIAL EQUIPMENT

Outdoor grill

1. Rinse the clams, discarding any with broken or open shells.

2. Preheat an outdoor grill to high heat.

3. Line a sheet pan or any grill-safe pan with ½ inch of kosher salt. Nestle the clams into the salt, leaving space between them.

4. Place the pan on the grill and close the lid. Grill until the clams open, 4 to 5 minutes. Remove the pan and place on a trivet for serving. Serve immediately with lemon wedges and hot sauce alongside.

HERB-CRUSTED YELLOWFIN TUNA

SERVES 4

5 tablespoons extra-virgin olive oil, plus more for drizzling

2 tablespoons good-quality soy sauce

1 tablespoon minced fresh ginger

4 yellowfin tuna steaks (7 ounces each), 1 inch thick, at room temperature

Fine sea salt and freshly ground white pepper

¼ cup herbes de Provence

2 cups mesclun

Canola oil for grilling

SPECIAL EQUIPMENT

Outdoor grill or stovetop grill pan

Pastry brush

Metal skewer

Here we use yellowfin tuna, but bluefin or bigeye are also excellent as their meaty texture lends itself well to grilling. Cut the tuna to a 1-inch thickness—anything bigger causes the crust to become too dry and the middle too cold. The tuna is best served warm and rare to medium-rare.

1. Preheat an outdoor grill or stovetop grill pan to high heat.

2. In a small bowl, whisk together the olive oil, soy sauce, and ginger. Set the dressing aside.

3. Season the tuna with sea salt and white pepper, then coat both sides with herbes de Provence, pressing firmly so that the herbs adhere. Lightly drizzle olive oil over the tuna.

4. Lightly season the mesclun with sea salt and white pepper, then toss it in a bowl with a few tablespoons of the dressing.

5. When the grill/pan is hot, use a pastry brush to apply a small amount of canola oil to the grate/pan. Place the steaks on the hot grill/pan and cook for 1 minute. Gently turn the fish over and cook for 1 minute more. A metal skewer inserted into the thickest part of the fish for 5 seconds should feel warm when touched to your wrist. Remove to a cutting board.

6. Using a very sharp knife, cut the tuna into ½-inch-thick slices. Evenly divide and fan the slices on four plates, then pile the salad next to the tuna. Spoon a little more dressing around the tuna and serve immediately.

CEDAR PLANK SALMON

SERVES 4

This dish is inspired by and evokes many memories of wonderful trips to the West Coast. The presentation is a little different from the usual cedar plank salmon recipe, but the most important part, the nice and distinctive flavor imparted by the cedar, is the same.

1 cup crème fraîche

2 tablespoons Dijon mustard

2 tablespoons whole-grain mustard

1 tablespoon red wine vinegar

Fine sea salt and freshly ground white pepper

4 salmon fillets (7 ounces each), skinned and pin bones removed

1. Rinse the cedar plank and soak it in warm water for at least 1 hour.

2. Preheat an outdoor grill to medium heat.

3. In a small saucepan, combine the crème fraîche, both mustards, and the vinegar and bring to a low simmer. Taste and season with sea salt and white pepper. Keep warm.

4. Season the salmon fillets on both sides with sea salt and white pepper.

5. Remove the cedar plank from the water and place it on the grill at least 6 inches from the heat source. Let it heat for 2 to 3 minutes, then place the salmon fillets on the plank and close the lid. Cook until a metal skewer inserted into the thickest part of the fish for 5 seconds feels warm when touched to your wrist, 9 to 10 minutes.

6. Divide the salmon fillets among four warm plates and serve with the warm mustard sauce.

SPECIAL EQUIPMENT

1 cedar plank

Outdoor grill

Metal skewer

SWORDFISH WITH CHIMICHURRI

SERVES 4

½ cup finely chopped fresh flat-leaf parsley

2 garlic cloves, minced

1 tablespoon minced onion

1 tablespoon finely chopped fresh oregano

3 tablespoons red wine vinegar

Fine sea salt and freshly ground white pepper

½ cup extra-virgin olive oil

4 boneless swordfish steaks (7 ounces each), skinned

Canola oil for grilling

Juice of ½ lime

SPECIAL EQUIPMENT

Outdoor grill or stovetop grill pan

Pastry brush

Metal skewer

Making the chimichurri a day in advance really brings out the flavors and aromatics of the herbs. I most enjoy swordfish cooked medium-rare, and I recommend a side of french fries with this dish.

1. In a bowl, combine the parsley, garlic, onion, oregano, and vinegar and season with sea salt and white pepper. Stir in the olive oil. Cover the chimichurri and keep cool, or preferably refrigerate overnight in an airtight container.

2. Preheat an outdoor grill or stovetop grill pan to high heat.

3. Season the swordfish steaks on both sides with sea salt and white pepper. When the grill/pan is hot, use a pastry brush to apply a small amount of canola oil to the grate/pan. Place a few drops of canola oil on the swordfish steaks and rub to coat.

4. Place the swordfish steaks on the grill/pan and cook without moving for 2 minutes. With a spatula, gently lift the fish and rotate it 90 degrees. Cook for another minute. Turn the steaks over and repeat, cooking for 2 minutes, then rotating the fish 90 degrees and cooking for 1 more minute. The fish is done when a metal skewer inserted into the thickest part of the fish for 5 seconds feels warm when touched to your wrist.

5. Remove the steaks to warm plates. Stir the lime juice into the chimichurri, then spoon the sauce over and around the steaks. Serve immediately.

SHRIMP SKEWERS
WITH GREEN CURRY SAUCE
SERVES 4

I like to serve the shrimp with the tails on, mostly for aesthetics, but you can remove them if you wish. Pineapple goes really well here, but you can swap it out for cantaloupe or even mango if you prefer.

1. Soak 16 bamboo skewers in warm water for a minimum of 15 minutes and up to 1 hour.

2. Nestle one cube of pineapple inside the curve of each shrimp. Thread two skewers through the top of the shrimp, through the pineapple, and then out through the tail. (See photo opposite.) Repeat twice more per each set of skewers. Each double skewer should hold 3 shrimp and 3 pineapple cubes. Refrigerate until ready to cook.

3. Make the curry sauce: In a medium saucepan, heat the canola oil over medium heat. Add the onion, garlic, and ginger and cook for 2 minutes, making sure not to brown them and turning the heat down as needed to avoid color. Add the lemongrass and sauté for 1 minute. Add the green curry paste and cook for 1 minute more. Stir in the tomato and cook for 2 to 3 minutes, until soft.

4. Stir in the coconut milk, lime zest, and ¼ cup water and bring to a simmer. Cook for 10 minutes to infuse the flavors. Strain through a fine-mesh sieve into a clean saucepan, pressing on the aromatics to extract their liquid. Season with the sea salt and white pepper to taste. Set aside and keep warm.

5. To finish: Preheat an outdoor grill or stovetop grill pan to medium heat.

6. Season the shrimp skewers with the cayenne and sea salt and freshly ground white pepper to taste.

7. When the grill/pan is hot, use a pastry brush to apply a small amount of canola oil to the grate/pan.

Recipe continues

24 cubes (1-inch) fresh pineapple

24 extra jumbo shrimp (16/20 count), peeled and deveined

CURRY SAUCE

1½ tablespoons canola oil

2 tablespoons chopped onion

1 tablespoon chopped garlic

1 tablespoon chopped fresh ginger

1 stalk lemongrass, trimmed and chopped

2 tablespoons Thai green curry paste

½ cup chopped tomato

1½ cups full-fat unsweetened coconut milk

Grated zest of 1 lime

1½ teaspoons fine sea salt

Freshly ground white pepper

TO FINISH

Pinch of cayenne pepper

Fine sea salt and freshly ground white pepper

Canola oil for grilling

SPECIAL EQUIPMENT

16 bamboo skewers

Outdoor grill or stovetop grill pan

Pastry brush

GRILLED

8. Place the skewers on the grill/pan and cook for 1 minute. (Cook in batches if all skewers will not fit on your grill pan.) Using a spatula or tongs, lift the skewers and rotate them 90 degrees. Cook for 30 to 60 seconds. Turn the shrimp over and repeat, cooking for 1 minute and then rotating the skewers 90 degrees and cooking until the shrimp are opaque, 1 minute longer.

9. Remove to a platter. Serve with hot curry sauce on the side.

BRANZINO
WITH CITRUS-FLAVORED EXTRA-VIRGIN OLIVE OIL
SERVES 4

The beauty of this dish is that the citrus oil can be made in advance and becomes more flavorful the longer it sits; just be sure to keep it tightly covered and refrigerated. When cooking the branzino, make sure the grill marks aren't too dark, as that can give the fish a bitter taste. I often add a splash of lemon juice at the end of the cooking process.

2 very ripe medium tomatoes

Fine sea salt and freshly ground black pepper

1½ teaspoons herbes de Provence

Canola oil

4 skin-on branzino fillets (7 ounces each)

Freshly ground white pepper

Citrus Oil (page 243) for serving

SPECIAL EQUIPMENT

Outdoor grill or stovetop grill pan

Pastry brush

Metal skewer

1. Halve each tomato horizontally through the equator and core them.

2. Set the tomato halves on a plate, cut side up, and season with sea salt and black pepper. Sprinkle with the herbes de Provence.

3. In a large nonstick skillet, heat 1 tablespoon canola oil over medium-high heat. Add the tomatoes, herb side down, and cook (gradually reducing the heat to avoid burning the herbs) until starting to brown, 2 to 3 minutes. Flip the tomatoes and cook for 1 more minute, until warm. Transfer to a plate.

4. Season the branzino fillets on both sides with sea salt and white pepper.

5. Preheat an outdoor grill or stovetop grill pan to medium-high heat.

6. When the grill/pan is hot, use a pastry brush to apply a small amount of canola oil to the grate/pan.

7. Gently pat the skin sides of the fillets dry to remove any moisture. Using a pastry brush, apply a small amount of canola oil on the skin side of each fillet.

8. Place the fillets skin side down on the grill/pan and cook for 2 minutes without moving. Using a spatula, gently lift the fish and rotate it 90 degrees. If the fish is sticking, let it cook for an additional

Recipe continues

minute and it should release. Continue to cook after rotating until the fish is slightly opaque, 3 to 4 minutes.

9. Gently turn the fish over and cook until a metal skewer inserted into the thickest part of the fish for 5 seconds feels warm when touched to your wrist, 20 to 30 seconds.

10. Remove the fillets to plates and serve with warm tomatoes and citrus oil on the side.

CITRUS OIL
MAKES APPROXIMATELY 1 CUP

Pour the olive oil into a bowl. Rub the thyme and rosemary leaves between your fingers, then add them to the oil. Stir in the zest strips and garlic and season to taste with sea salt and white pepper. Extra oil can be stored in an airtight container in the refrigerator for up to 3 days.

1 cup extra-virgin olive oil

5 sprigs thyme, leaves picked

1 sprig rosemary, leaves picked

3 × 1-inch strip orange zest, fine julienned

3 × 1-inch strip lemon zest, fine julienned

3 × 1-inch strip lime zest, fine julienned

2 garlic cloves, halved lengthwise

Fine sea salt and freshly ground white pepper

MARINATED MAHIMAHI KEBABS

SERVES 4

2 pounds mahimahi, cut into 1-inch cubes

1 small zucchini (about 1 inch in diameter), cut into ¼-inch-thick slices

1 small yellow squash (about 1 inch in diameter), cut into ¼-inch-thick slices

½ cup extra-virgin olive oil

4 garlic cloves, halved

2 tablespoons herbes de Provence

1 teaspoon cayenne pepper

Canola oil for grilling

Fine sea salt and freshly ground white pepper

1 lemon, halved and seeded

SPECIAL EQUIPMENT

8 bamboo skewers

Outdoor grill or stovetop grill pan

Pastry brush

Metal skewer

Mahimahi must be cooked quickly to avoid drying it out, making quick-cooking kebabs a good choice. Select small zucchini and squash so that they cook in the same amount of time as the fish. I like to eat these kebabs in the summer with a simple green salad.

1. Soak 8 bamboo skewers in warm water for a minimum of 15 minutes and up to 1 hour.

2. Make sure the fish and vegetables are all cut to a similar size so they cook evenly. This will also help them lie flat on the grill.

3. In a large bowl, combine the extra-virgin olive oil, garlic, herbes de Provence, and cayenne. Measure out ¼ cup of the marinade and set aside for later. Add the mahimahi and all the vegetables to the bowl and toss to coat. Refrigerate for 30 minutes or up to 1 hour.

4. Thread the mahimahi and vegetables onto the skewers, alternating pieces of zucchini, squash, and mahimahi.

5. Preheat an outdoor grill or stovetop grill pan to medium-high heat.

6. When the grill/pan is hot, use a pastry brush to apply a small amount of canola oil to the grate/pan.

7. Season the kebabs with sea salt and white pepper. Place them on the grill/pan and grill until well browned, 2 to 3 minutes. Carefully turn the skewers over and cook until a metal skewer inserted into the thickest part of the fish for 5 seconds feels warm when touched to your wrist, another 2 to 3 minutes.

8. Remove the kebabs to a serving platter and squeeze the lemon juice over them. Top with the reserved marinade. Let rest for a few minutes to cool and then serve.

SNOW CRAB
WITH MELTED BUTTER

SERVES 4

Snow crab legs are easy to crack—just let them cool after taking them off the grill and use your hands to break them open and pull the flesh out. If the legs are still attached to a piece of the crab's body, use scissors to cut it open—there is plenty of meat in there, too. Grilling the crab legs as you go makes for a fun, rustic, and convivial meal, and I love enjoying them outside in the summer around a table with cold beer or wine and good friends.

1. Preheat an outdoor grill to medium-high heat.

2. In a saucepan, bring the butter to a simmer over medium heat, skimming any foam off the top. Transfer to a bowl and keep warm.

3. When the grill is hot, use a pastry brush to apply a small amount of canola oil to the grate.

4. Place the crab legs on the grill and cook until their shells turn bright red, 5 to 6 minutes, turning halfway through. Remove to large plates to cool.

5. Once cool, crack the legs open using your hands or a small mallet, or cut them open with shears. Serve immediately with the melted butter.

1 stick (4 ounces) unsalted butter

Canola oil for grilling

4 to 5 pounds snow crab or queen crab legs, thawed if frozen

SPECIAL EQUIPMENT

Outdoor grill

Pastry brush

Mallet

LOBSTER
WITH GREEN BUTTER SAUCE
SERVES 4

1 stick (4 ounces) unsalted butter, at room temperature

2 tablespoons finely sliced fresh chives

1 tablespoon finely chopped fresh flat-leaf parsley

1 teaspoon minced garlic

1 teaspoon grated lemon zest

1 tablespoon fresh lemon juice

Fine sea salt and freshly ground white pepper

4 live lobsters (1¾ pounds each)

Canola oil for grilling

SPECIAL EQUIPMENT

Outdoor grill with cover

Pastry brush

Uncooked, a lobster shell has a dark, bluish color that turns red when cooked and adds intensity to its flavor. I recommend covering the lobster when grilling so that it cooks well and evenly. Let the lobster rest for a minute or two before serving to allow the flesh to settle.

1. In a bowl, combine the softened butter, chives, parsley, garlic, lemon zest, and lemon juice and mix well. Season lightly with sea salt and white pepper. Cover and refrigerate.

2. Preheat an outdoor grill to medium-high heat.

3. Place a lobster belly down on a cutting board. Place the tip of a sharp knife in the center of the head with the blade pointing toward the front of the head. Press down, splitting the head in two; this will kill the lobster quickly. (See How to Split a Lobster, page 12, for photos, but leave the claws on the body.)

4. Lay the lobster on the cutting board with its belly side facing up. Starting from where the head meets the tail, cut 90 percent of the way through the body, leaving the outer shell intact, continuing through the tail. Turn the lobster 180 degrees and continue cutting through the head. Holding the lobster in your hands, open it like a book to expose the flesh. Gently wash the head section and remove if not desired.

5. When the grill is hot, use a pastry brush to apply a small amount of canola oil to the grate. Place the lobsters directly on the grate, shell side down. Cover the grill and cook until the shells turn bright red and the tail meat has firmed up, 6 to 8 minutes. Remove from the grill and let rest for 4 to 5 minutes, until cool enough to handle.

6. Using the back of a knife or scissors, crack open the claws. Transfer the lobsters to plates and serve with the green butter alongside.

SALMON WITH PEAS AND BACON

SERVES 4

This dish is delicious at the beginning of spring when peas are most tender. If you can't find fresh peas, good-quality frozen baby or English peas work great, too. If you like smokiness, you can use smoked bacon, and for added crunch, chopped raw snow peas. Sometimes, if I have some peppermint on hand, I thinly julienne it and sprinkle it on the peas last minute.

4 slices thick-cut bacon, cut into ¼-inch dice

1½ cups fresh or frozen peas

Fine sea salt and freshly ground white pepper

4 salmon fillets (7 ounces each), skinned and pin bones removed

Canola oil for grilling

SPECIAL EQUIPMENT

Outdoor grill or stovetop grill pan

Pastry brush

Metal skewer

1. Line a plate with paper towels. In a large skillet, cook the bacon over medium heat, stirring occasionally, for 5 to 6 minutes, until the fat is rendered and the bacon is crisp. Transfer the bacon to the paper towels to drain.

2. Pour off all but 1 tablespoon of the bacon fat from the pan and return it to the heat. Add the peas and cook until tender, 4 to 5 minutes. Season with sea salt and white pepper.

3. Preheat the grill or a grill pan to medium-high heat.

4. Season the salmon fillets on both sides with sea salt and white pepper and set aside.

5. When the grill/pan is hot, use a pastry brush to apply a small amount of canola oil to the grate/pan. Pat the fish dry to remove any excess moisture, then rub with a small amount of canola oil.

6. Lay the fish on the grill/pan and cook for 2 to 3 minutes. Using a spatula, gently lift the fish and rotate it 90 degrees. Cook for an additional 1 to 2 minutes. Gently turn the fish over and cook until a metal skewer inserted into the thickest part of the fish for 5 seconds feels warm when touched to your wrist, about 1 minute longer.

7. Quickly rewarm the peas, stir in the reserved bacon, and serve alongside the grilled salmon.

PRESERVED

PRESERVE

To prepare food for long storage through various methods such as curing, tinning/canning, freezing, pickling, and smoking

Today you can easily find a wide variety of high-quality canned seafood such as tuna, sardines, mussels, and clams, among many others, in most grocery stores. In Spain, every good tapas bar offers these pleasures, sometimes even simply served as is, in the can.

If you want to experiment and make your own, I recommend starting with albacore tuna. It's incredibly versatile, a champion staple for your refrigerator, and a great string to add to your bow of accomplished recipes.

PRESSURE-CANNED ALBACORE TUNA

MAKES 1 POUND

While you can purchase good-quality canned albacore tuna at the store, it's a fun and easy recipe to do at home. With the seal intact, this version can keep up to 2 months in the fridge. Once the seal is opened, use the tuna within 3 days. This recipe is for 1 pound of tuna, but it can easily be scaled up.

1 pound albacore tuna loin

¾ teaspoon fine sea salt

¼ teaspoon freshly ground white pepper

1 shallot, cut into rings

Extra-virgin olive oil

SPECIAL EQUIPMENT

2 wide-mouthed 1-pint canning jars

Pressure cooker

1. Remove any bones from the tuna and cut it into similarly sized pieces that will fit in the pint jars, about 4 × 1 × 1 inch.

2. Season the tuna with the sea salt and white pepper, then refrigerate for 1 hour.

3. Make sure the jars are clean and dry, following proper sterilization procedures.

4. Place 1 shallot ring at the bottom of each jar, then fill them one-quarter of the way full with olive oil.

5. Pack the tuna pieces lengthwise into the jars.

6. Cover with olive oil, leaving about ½ inch of room at the top for the contents of the jar to expand.

7. Tap the jars on the counter to remove any trapped air. Place the lids and screw bands on the jars and tighten by hand.

8. Put the jars in a pressure cooker and fill with 2 inches of water. Close and seal the pressure cooker and bring to 15 pounds of pressure according to the manufacturer's directions. Pressure cook at that pressure for 7 minutes. Remove from the heat and let the pressure cooker depressurize completely.

9. Once depressurized, remove the jars from the cooker and let rest until they are at room temperature. Refrigerate for up to 2 months if sealed; once the seal is broken, use within 3 days.

SARDINE TARTINES

SERVES 4

2 tins high-quality oil-packed sardines

4 tablespoons unsalted butter, at room temperature

8 slices sourdough bread, toasted

Canned sardines are a wonderful ingredient to have on hand as they store easily, don't need to be refrigerated, and keep for a very long time. In Europe, there's a growing trend to age sardines in oil and sell them as a delicacy. I like to buy them already deboned and eat them on toasted bread with butter as a snack.

Open the tins and serve sardines with softened butter on toasted sourdough.

ALBACORE TUNA TARTINES

SERVES 6

Canned tuna is a great resource to keep in your cupboard. You can make your own, as I like to do (see Pressure-Canned Albacore Tuna, page 257), or seek out a good-quality canned tuna packed in olive oil. I enjoy it mixed with mustard and mayo in salads and sandwiches, or on top of crackers or mini toasts. I drain the oil from the tuna before using, and sometimes keep it to add to dressings or to drizzle over bread.

8 ounces olive oil–packed canned albacore tuna, homemade or good-quality store-bought

Extra-virgin olive oil (optional)

1½ teaspoons Dijon mustard

1 baguette, cut crosswise into 6-inch lengths and split horizontally

12 (¼-inch-thick) half-moons cucumber

½ small red onion, thinly sliced

½ red bell pepper, thinly sliced

4 kalamata olives, pitted and quartered

1. If your tuna is homemade and refrigerated, let it come to room temperature.

2. Preheat the oven to 400°F.

3. Reserving the oil, drain the tuna. (If using store-bought tuna and you don't have ¼ cup of oil, supplement with extra-virgin olive oil.) Put the mustard in a medium bowl, then whisk in the ¼ cup reserved oil to emulsify. Gently fold in the tuna, keeping it in large chunks; do not overmix. Set aside.

4. Toast the baguette pieces in the oven until light golden brown, 3 to 4 minutes.

5. Moisten each toast with a splash of oil from the tuna jar (or olive oil) and top with the tuna mixture. (Refrigerate any leftover canned tuna oil for another use.) Garnish with slices of cucumber, red onion, bell pepper, and olives. Serve immediately.

BOQUERONES CAESAR SALAD

SERVES 4

4 teaspoons red wine vinegar

1 garlic clove, finely chopped

1 teaspoon anchovy paste

1 teaspoon Dijon mustard

Fine sea salt

½ cup extra-virgin olive oil

⅓ cup grated parmesan cheese

1 large head romaine lettuce, quartered lengthwise

24 boquerones fillets, bones removed

SPECIAL EQUIPMENT

Pastry brush

Originating in Spain and traditionally served as tapas, boquerones are anchovies that have been lightly pickled, usually in white wine vinegar, and stored in the refrigerator. I particularly enjoy them simply drizzled with olive oil and sprinkled with some freshly ground black pepper, which on first bite, immediately transports me back to my childhood.

1. In a small bowl, combine the vinegar, garlic, anchovy paste, and mustard and whisk to combine. Season lightly with sea salt. Slowly whisk in the olive oil to emulsify the Caesar vinaigrette.

2. Using a pastry brush, coat the romaine quarters inside and out with the Caesar vinaigrette, then sprinkle with the parmesan.

3. Drape 5 or 6 boquerones fillets crosswise over the top of each lettuce quarter and serve immediately.

TIPS & GUIDELINES

Seafood is an umbrella term for two main categories: fish and shell-fish. And those categories can be broken down even further.

FISH

In basic terms, fish have gills, fins, and a bone structure. There are tens of thousands of species of fish, and they are generally separated into two groups: freshwater fish and saltwater fish. These fish are divided even further into two more categories based on their shape: flatfish and roundfish.

SHELLFISH

As the name suggests, shellfish are sea creatures that have an outer shell of some kind, which are classified into two groups: crustaceans and mollusks. Crustaceans include lobster, shrimp, and crab. Mollusks include three groups: bivalves (such as oysters, scallops, mussels, and clams), gastropods (such as whelks), and cephalopods (such as octopus and squid), which do not in fact have shells.

Fish and shellfish are handled differently when it comes to sourcing, storing, prepping, and cooking, and the following guidelines are a general overview of the best practices to undertake when working with seafood.

SEASONS / SEASONALITY

Bivalves, including oysters, clams, and mussels, are at their best in the cooler months. A common way to remember when it is best to eat oysters is the "rule of r," which states that they should be eaten raw only in the months that contain the letter r, that is, from September through April. The warmer months of May, June, July, and August are spawning season for oysters (as well as clams and mussels), and during this period their flesh takes on a milky texture and isn't as firm or as flavorful as it is when they are in colder waters.

Crustaceans such as shrimp, lobster, and crab can be enjoyed all year round, but it is important to note that shellfish should not be caught during the shedding and spawning months of spring and summer because of sustainability and legality. In addition to these important reasons, their flesh is not as firm during this period.

Due to the wide variety and migration habits of fish, there will be good-quality options available all year long. Popular migrating fish include tuna, swordfish, and striped bass. Always check with your fishmonger to see what is currently, and locally, in season. The market price for fish in season is always favorable to the consumer.

FARM-RAISED VS WILD-CAUGHT

This is a common question when discussing seafood, and one with no quick or easy answer. There are many pros and cons, benefits and weaknesses to both farm-raised and wild-caught seafood, and understanding these will hopefully help you make an informed decision about what is best for you.

Farmed fish are commercially produced via aquaculture in dedicated contained environments (such as enclosures, pens, and tanks) in our oceans, rivers, and freshwater bodies.

In general, I prefer to use wild-caught seafood when I can. I would rather support sustainable fishing practices in the wild; however, I do recognize that fish farming has evolved tremendously, and today we have easy access to farmed fish that's fresh, easy to trace, and has good flavor thanks to these fish farmers undertaking better commercial practices. Farmed fish are often less expensive than wild and are more readily available. However, their flavor isn't as refined, mainly due to the food they are given, which tends to be made of inexpensive ingredients that are inferior to the natural food sources consumed by fish in the wild. Due to the fact that farmed fish live in contained spaces, they are given antibiotics to prevent disease, and often growth hormones as well. Some are even genetically modified.

As implied by their name, wild-caught fish are caught in their natural environments. As a chef specializing in seafood, I prefer wild-caught fish over farm-raised because they have better flavor (due to their more natural diet) and no exposure to antibiotics. Aside from the flavor profile, purchasing responsibly wild-caught fish encourages sustainability as well as supports smaller fishermen communities. Wild-caught fish are not without their challenges, though. They are more expensive and can be exposed to pollution and contaminants, especially mercury, and demand for wild-caught fish in some instances has caused overfishing of certain species.

To keep informed and up to date on best practices with regard to fishing industry regulations, marine ecosystems, and sustainability, I find NOAA (National Oceanic and Atmospheric Administration) to be one of the best educational resources—at least for those based in the United States. I tend to follow their guidelines not only as a chef and restaurateur but also for my own sense of personal responsibility.

SOURCING / SHOPPING

My first piece of advice when sourcing and shopping for seafood is to find an experienced, trustworthy fishmonger and develop a good relationship with them. When possible, I highly recommend purchasing your seafood the same day you are planning to cook it. As mentioned previously, not all seafood is treated the same in terms of handling, availability, etc. While the following information is a strong general, topline guide for sourcing various categories of seafood—bivalves, crustaceans, fish (whole and fillets)—I do recommend discussing your specific needs with your fishmonger. The one shopping test that applies to all seafood is the smell test. I cannot overstate how important it is to really lean into the power of smell to differentiate between seafood that's fresh and seafood that is past its prime. A "fishy" odor is *never* good. Fresh fish and seafood should always evoke the smell of a clean, fresh ocean breeze, or high tide as I like to describe it.

BIVALVES

When purchasing clams, oysters, mussels, scallops, and other bivalves, make sure they are washed, closed, and not damaged or cracked. They should be weighty, indicating the presence of seawater, and should have that fresh, clean smell of the sea.

CRUSTACEANS

Lobsters, if bought fresh, should be very much alive, otherwise their flesh will have a mealy, mushy, and soft texture.

Most shrimp you find in markets have been frozen and left to thaw, so when purchasing these I recommend buying them with their shells on. Their shells should be nice and bright and their flesh firm and translucent—if they are in any way opaque or dry, it means they are old or have been damaged or burned by ice.

FISH

Fish are primarily available in two forms: whole or fillets.

Whole fish

There are several ways beyond the initial smell test to determine if a whole fish is fresh. Check the eyes: The eyes in a fresh whole fish should be clear and not cloudy or sunken. If the fish has gills, they should be a bright, vibrant red. Touch the flesh: If it's fresh fish, it should always spring back when pressed gently. If the fish has scales, they should be difficult to pull off. Finish your checklist with another smell test, but this time, do so once the fish has been gutted or cleaned, and smell the belly—even the slightest hint of unpleasant-ness means it isn't fresh.

 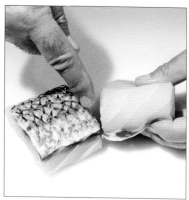

Fillets

With fillets (and other cut fish like steaks and loins), because the flesh of the fish is exposed, it's important to pay attention to, and understand, its color and texture. The flesh of fresh white fish should be vibrant, almost translucent, tight, and undamaged. Its skin shouldn't be dull or dry, and any visible blood vessels should be very red—brown indicates that the blood has oxidized, meaning it has been exposed for a while.

While most salmon you find at the market is farm-raised, its unique orangey-pink hue should still be vivid and rich. On the contrary, tuna's ruby-red color shouldn't be too red, as that suggests that the blood hasn't been drained properly, and thus it will carry a very strong fish flavor. If the flesh is dull or has a brown tint, it means it's old or has been handled improperly.

STORAGE

Seafood is delicate, and its flavor and texture change drastically when not kept at very cold temperatures or if stored incorrectly. Even though I strongly recommend buying your seafood the day you plan to prepare and serve it, you still need to store it correctly, and, in some cases, storing it correctly may even extend its shelf life a little.

Fish is best stored wrapped in parchment paper and kept on or over ice, but it's important that the flesh not come in direct contact with the ice. Keep it in a very cold place, at around 35°F so as to avoid freezer burn. If you purchased the fish whole, it needs to be cleaned (gutted and gills removed) before storing it. Shrimp and calamari should be stored the same way.

Live lobsters shouldn't be stored in water, but covered with a wet towel with their tails curled beneath them and kept chilled before cooking.

Oysters, clams, and mussels should be placed in an open-top plastic or glass container, covered with a wet towel, and kept in the coldest part of the fridge. Oysters and clams especially should be stacked on top of one another, rounded belly side down and flat side up to prevent their liquid from seeping out of their shells.

FREEZING

If you decide to freeze fish, make sure the fillets or pieces are individually wrapped in parchment paper and then overwrapped in plastic. Lay them flat in the freezer, and don't keep them longer than a few weeks as they will start to lose moisture and flavor and will become susceptible to freezer burn. If freezing lobster, separate the tails from the heads. Like fish, make sure the lobster tails are individually wrapped. The frozen heads can be used to make stock and sauces. If you have bought frozen fish or shellfish (such as shrimp), never refreeze them after thawing. Never ever freeze bivalves (oysters, clams, mussels). Thaw frozen seafood slowly in the refrigerator for a few hours or even overnight.

CAVIAR AND OTHER FISH ROES

Caviar is salted fish eggs or roe, with the "best" considered to be from wild sturgeon found in the Caspian and the Black Seas. The three kinds of sturgeon caviar are beluga, osetra, and sevruga, and they are also the costliest. Today, in America, we no longer have access to these caviars, but we can find good farm-raised caviar that is a close cousin of wild osetra.

Caviar is not supposed to be overly salty, bitter, or have a muddy or metallic flavor. It should be only slightly salty, with nutty and briny undertones. The grains (or pearls) can have many assorted colors ranging from rich golden hues to light and dark grays and blacks. The color doesn't have too much influence on flavor, so don't get bogged down on that aspect when you are shopping. What is important is the consistency; it shouldn't be too soft nor too hard and never mushy or oily—you want to be able to see the pearls clearly defined.

Salmon, trout, and other fish roes are more affordable alternatives, and they have the same characteristics as sturgeon caviar, so you should follow the same guidelines and observations with regard to taste and consistency.

When caviar is served as a stand-alone appetizer, it's usually accompanied by blinis and crème fraîche. Traditionally, it would have been served with a selection of condiments and garnishes, including hard-boiled egg yolks and whites, chives or minced onion, capers, cornichons, parsley, and lemon wedges; however, this was mostly done a long time ago to mask the strong flavor. These days, good caviar has such a subtle and delicate flavor that I personally prefer to enjoy it on its own or with a little crème fraîche. If you are cooking with caviar or using it as a component for a dish (such as the Smoked Salmon "Croque-Monsieur," page 177), make sure that it gets only barely warm; if it passes that point, it will be cooked and therefore hard and too salty.

Buying caviar and roes for the first time can be intimidating, but don't be afraid to ask to try it first. It's important to taste it before bringing it home, and good sellers are happy to oblige. I recommend buying caviar as close to the time you are planning to use it as possible. Store it in the coldest part of the refrigerator, but never freeze it. When you open the tin, make sure you eat within 24 hours.

ACKNOWLEDGMENTS

Seafood Simple is my eighth book, and I have found my appreciation for the work, time, and sacrifice undertaken by those involved in such projects only grows and grows. I am incredibly lucky, especially given the turmoil of these pandemic years, to have the same team work with me on *Seafood Simple* as I did on my previous book, *Vegetable Simple*. Producing a cookbook, or any book for that matter, is no easy feat, and I have been blessed with an exceptionally talented bunch. From the bottom of my heart and the depths of my gratitude, I would like to recognize and thank the following:

My not-just-my-agent agent, Kim Witherspoon. Kim has been an ardent advocate and fierce champion of me and my ideas for as long as I can remember. I strive to be as steadfast as she, and as good a friend.

Andy Ward, and his A team at Random House. They are quite literally the best in the business, and I am forever grateful to him for his belief in me, his invaluable advice and guidance, and his commitment to making *Seafood Simple* a reality. Particular gratitude to Clio Seraphim for her grace in editing.

Nigel Parry, longtime dear friend and world-renowned photographer, who humored me for the second time by agreeing to shift gears from his prolific portrait work to collaborate again to make food his subject. The process was both fun and profound, and his images are nothing short of art.

Cathy Sheary, former "Le Bernardin guardian angel," dear friend, and eloquent writer who made it possible to translate my ideas onto the page.

Erik Fricker, our researcher and developer and right hand for recipes. I'm eternally grateful for his tireless commitment to this book as well as his demanding day job as a sous-chef at Le Bernardin.

Laura Russell for her time, hard work, care, and diligence in testing and organizing these recipes.

My Le Bernardin family, who, no matter how busy they are, will always make room and find time to allow me to work on projects such as this book and keep the restaurant running at full speed. I'm honored to stand with you every day. A special thanks to Remy Albert for her dedication and loyalty, and for keeping me on track and on schedule.

My wife, Sandra; son, Adrien; my mother; and my extended family, whose patience, understanding, and love inspire me each and every day, and I hope I return it tenfold.

Maguy Le Coze, for her unquestionable faith, support, and perpetual friendship.

My mentors for their lifelong inspiration, education, and motivation.

INDEX

ABOUT THE TYPE

This book was set in Fournier, a typeface named for Pierre-Simon Fournier (1712–68), the youngest son of a French printing family. He started out engraving woodblocks and large capitals, then moved on to fonts of type. In 1736 he began his own foundry and made several important contributions in the field of type design; he is said to have cut 147 alphabets of his own creation. Fournier is probably best remembered as the designer of St. Augustine Ordinaire, a face that served as the model for the Monotype Corporation's Fournier, which was released in 1925.